WOMAN'S REALM
CAKE ICING

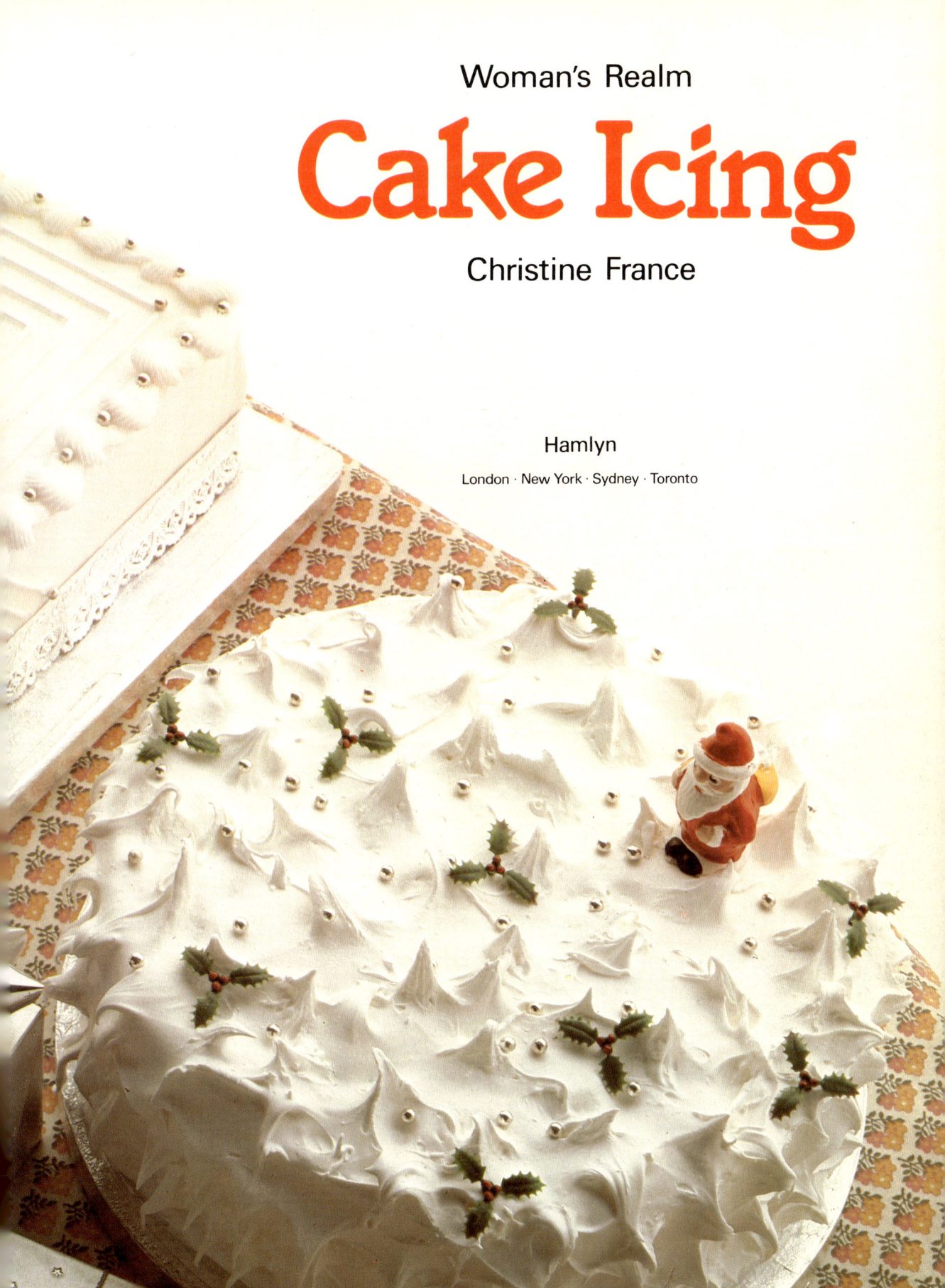

Woman's Realm

Cake Icing

Christine France

Hamlyn
London · New York · Sydney · Toronto

Photography by Paul Williams
Illustrations by Roberta Colegate-Stone
Endpapers in New England design by
Juliet Glynn Smith
© 1976 Hunkydory Designs Limited

Published by The Hamlyn Publishing Group Limited
London · New York · Sydney · Toronto
Astronaut House, Feltham, Middlesex, England

Third impression 1984

© Copyright The Hamlyn Publishing Group Limited 1982

ISBN 0 600 32270 X

All rights reserved. No part of this publication may
be reproduced, stored in a retrieval system, or transmitted
in any form or by any means, electronic, mechanical, photocopying,
recording or otherwise, without the permission of
The Hamlyn Publishing Group Limited.

Phototypeset in 10/11 pt Monophoto Garamond by
Tameside Filmsetting Limited, Ashton-under-Lyne, Lancashire

Printed in the Canary Islands (Spain)
by Litografía A. Romero, S.A.
D. L. TF. 1.355 - 1982

Contents

Introduction	11
Useful Facts and Figures	12
Useful Equipment	13
Cake Recipes	19
Icings and Fillings	27
Basic Techniques	35
Iced Cakes for all Occasions	57
Teatime Cakes	58
Gâteaux	69
Celebration Cakes	73
Formal Cakes	92
Children's Party Cakes	112
Index	123
Acknowledgements	125
Useful Addresses	125

Introduction

Good quality iced cakes are extremely difficult to find and expensive to buy, so a little time spent learning the techniques of icing at home is both rewarding and worthwhile.

Most cake icing does not, in fact, demand a very high degree of skill – just enthusiasm and patience, with a little time and trouble. Even the most inexperienced cook aspires to create impressive confections for special occasions. And there are times, too, when a more experienced and ambitious cook simply needs to put together a basic iced sponge quickly with the maximum effect. This book is designed to serve both purposes.

Beginning with detailed information on the equipment you need (and how to improvise if you have not got it), I have gone on to give basic recipes for cakes, icings and fillings before starting on the icing techniques themselves. These have been covered as clearly and comprehensively as possible, from simple flooding with glacé icing to the more sophisticated royal icing techniques, such as making flowers and piping trellis work. Each technique is illustrated with clear step-by-step drawings; follow these closely, practising them first if you are a beginner, and the whole world of cake icing and decorating is open to you.

The main part of the book then gives you the chance to put all the first four sections together in perfecting the teatime treats and special occasion cakes – over 40 of them – specially designed for you to try.

Even if you've never iced a cake before, with the right guidance you'll be surprised what you can achieve. In fact, a totally unskilled cook can often find in cake icing a talent till then untapped. For a more confident cake icer, this book will provide a useful reference, as the ideas I have used can be adapted and interpreted to suit individual tastes and needs.

All cooking requires confidence before it can become fun. And when you gain confidence, I hope you too will discover that cake icing is not only satisfying and enjoyable, but a release for creative ideas which are your very own.

I would like to thank Jane Suthering for all her help and hard work throughout the making of this book, and Roberta Colegate-Stone for the very attractive and useful illustrations.

Christine France

Useful Facts and Figures

Notes on metrication
In this book quantities are given in metric and Imperial measures. Exact conversion from Imperial to metric measures does not usually give very convenient working quantities and so the metric measures have been rounded off into units of 25 grams. The table below shows the recommended equivalents.

Ounces	Approx g to nearest whole figure	Recommended conversion to nearest unit of 25
1	28	25
2	57	50
3	85	75
4	113	100
5	142	150
6	170	175
7	198	200
8	227	225
9	255	250
10	283	275
11	312	300
12	340	350
13	368	375
14	396	400
15	425	425
16 (1 lb)	454	450
17	482	475
18	510	500
19	539	550
20 (1¼ lb)	567	575

Note When converting quantities over 20 oz first add the appropriate figures in the centre column, then adjust to the nearest unit of 25. As a general guide, 1 kg (1000 g) equals 2.2 lb or about 2 lb 3 oz. This method of conversion gives good results in nearly all cases, although in certain pastry and cake recipes a more accurate conversion is necessary to produce a balanced recipe.

Liquid measures The millilitre has been used in this book and the following table gives a few examples.

Imperial	Approx ml to nearest whole figure	Recommended ml
¼ pint	142	150 ml
½ pint	283	300 ml
¾ pint	425	450 ml
1 pint	567	600 ml
1½ pints	851	900 ml
1¾ pints	992	1000 ml (1 litre)

Spoon measures All spoon measures given in this book are level unless otherwise stated.

Oven temperatures
The table below gives recommended equivalents.

	°C	°F	Gas Mark
Very cool	110	225	¼
	120	250	½
Cool	140	275	1
	150	300	2
Moderate	160	325	3
	180	350	4
Moderately hot	190	375	5
	200	400	6
Hot	220	425	7
	230	450	8
Very hot	240	475	9

Notes for American and Australian users
In America the 8-oz measuring cup is used. In Australia metric measures are now used in conjunction with the standard 250-ml measuring cup. The Imperial pint, used in Britain and Australia, is 20 fl oz, while the American pint is 16 fl oz. It is important to remember that the Australian tablespoon differs from both the British and American tablespoons; the table below gives a comparison. The British standard tablespoon, which has been used throughout this book, holds 17.7 ml, the American 14.2 ml, and the Australian 20 ml. A teaspoon holds approximately 5 ml in all three countries.

British	American	Australian
1 teaspoon	1 teaspoon	1 teaspoon
1 tablespoon	1 tablespoon	1 tablespoon
2 tablespoons	3 tablespoons	2 tablespoons
3½ tablespoons	4 tablespoons	3 tablespoons
4 tablespoons	5 tablespoons	3½ tablespoons

Imperial/American guide to solid measures

Imperial	American
1 lb butter or margarine	2 cups
1 lb flour	4 cups
1 lb granulated or castor sugar	2 cups
1 lb icing sugar	3 cups
8 oz rice	1 cup

Note: When making any of the recipes in this book, only follow one set of measures as they are not interchangeable.

Useful Equipment

Very few special tools are required for cake icing – most of the things you'll need are probably part of your standard kitchen equipment already.

These are some of the basic essentials:

Mixing bowls One large mixing bowl, two or three medium ones and one small one would be a good selection. Earthenware is perhaps the best material as it heats very evenly which is ideal for recipes that require the gentle melting of ingredients over a pan of hot water. Stainless steel is not so suitable for this as it heats very quickly, with the risk that the ingredients could spoil. Ovenproof glass and plastic make good mixing bowls, but care should be taken when using plastic over heat.

Spoons You will need two or three wooden spoons and one metal tablespoon. A wooden spoon is best for beating with – comfortable to use, its rounded edge helps to beat the air in. But a metal spoon is better for folding in ingredients such as flour or whisked egg white: the clean cutting edge prevents too much air escaping from a whipped-up, fluffy mixture.

Palette knife This knife consists of a long metal blade with a rounded tip, and is invaluable for applying icing to both top and sides of the cake. Use it with a smooth, sweeping action to eliminate air bubbles and give a smooth or patterned finish as required.

Spatula A plastic or rubber spatula is very useful for cleaning out the mixing bowl and ensuring that not a scrap of icing is wasted.

Sieve A wide-based nylon or wire mesh sieve is the easiest kind to use for sifting icing sugar. You can also use a conical sieve but this type is really intended for liquids and is not so effective with icing sugar.

Always sift into a wide-mouthed bowl to avoid spillage. The best method is to hold the sieve in one hand over the bowl and tap it lightly with the other hand. Coarse ingredients may have to be helped through the sieve with a wooden spoon.

Mixers and beaters An electric hand-held whisk is very useful, as several icing recipes call for vigorous whisking and this would aid you particularly in whisking ingredients in a bowl placed over a saucepan of hot water. A simple hand whisk would of course do the job, though in longer time. A food mixer is helpful for creaming butter and sugar but is by no means an essential item.

Rolling pin You will need this for rolling out almond paste and fondant.

USEFUL EQUIPMENT

Covers Icing must be kept covered, or it will quickly form a crust – even in the mixing bowl – before you have a chance to transfer it to the cake. Some plastic bowls come equipped with lids; otherwise use a damp tea towel.

Pastry brush Use a brush for greasing cake tins or spreading apricot glaze – it's the easiest way.

Containers You will need biscuit tins or large airtight plastic boxes in which to store cakes once they have been iced.

Special icing equipment

Cake cards and boards A firm base for the cake you are going to ice will make it easier to handle. A card or board base will also enhance the appearance of an iced cake, especially one for a festive occasion.

Cake cards, suitable for sponge cakes, are simply pieces of cardboard measuring about 3 mm/$\frac{1}{8}$ in thick and covered in silver or gold foil. Cake boards are also made of cardboard covered in gold or silver foil but are much thicker and stronger, measuring 1.3 cm/$\frac{5}{8}$ in. in depth. They are hollow inside, make good, firm bases for heavy fruit cakes, and can be used again and again, so long as they are not damaged when the cakes are cut. Simply wipe them carefully after use with a damp cloth.

Choose a card or board with a diameter 5 cm/2 in larger than the cake itself so that there is room for a border of icing to be piped round the base of the cake while still leaving a good proportion of the board to be seen. If you want to ice and decorate the board itself as part of the design, you may need an even larger one.

For less formal occasions you can make an improvised cake board from a chopping board covered with kitchen foil.

Turntables If you are planning to do much formal cake decoration it would be well worth your while to invest in a good turntable. Although it is perfectly possible to ice a stationary cake, it is very much easier if you can turn it

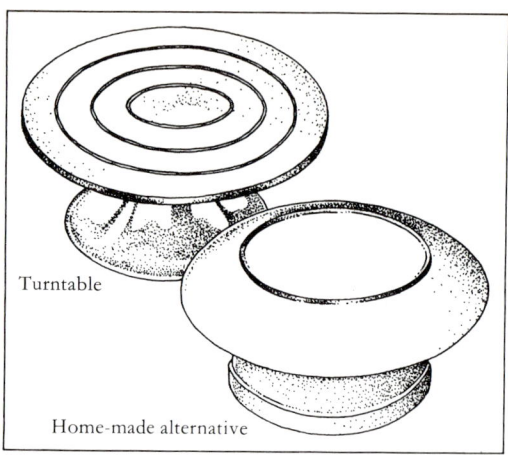

Turntable

Home-made alternative

gently with one hand while applying the icing with the other.

Turntables are made either of metal or of plastic and can be anything from 5 cm/2 in to 20 cm/8 in high. They consist of a heavy base and a flat, rotating top. Be sure to choose one with a firm, solid base which is well balanced so that it will not tip over, even when supporting a heavy cake.

You can construct your own turntable by placing a bowl upside down on your working surface and topping it with an upturned dinner plate on which you put the cake. This will only work if the inner rim of the plate exactly fits the shape of the bowl, so that the plate moves smoothly when you turn it.

Icing bags Nylon or plastic icing bags are best, as they are easily cleaned by washing in warm soapy water. Linen bags are also available, but they have to be boiled and dried thoroughly each time after use.

The size you choose will depend on the kind of icing you plan to do. A small icing bag is suitable for fine work in royal or glacé icing, such as lettering. A medium icing bag is best for the thicker kinds of icing – butter cream for instance. It can also be used for royal icing, but is not suitable for executing fine writing, as you would find the bag too big to handle easily. A large icing bag is used for piping butter icings, meringues, or cream.

You can make your own icing bag with greaseproof paper. This is simple to do, costs very little and, being disposable, doesn't have to be

USEFUL EQUIPMENT

washed. A greaseproof paper bag is quite good for fine icing if you are not using too large a quantity. It's comfortable to use, moulding easily to the shape of the hand, and can even be opened and refilled. Never fill it more than half full though; you should be left with a good proportion of greaseproof paper at the top to fold over and seal the bag, otherwise the icing might ooze out as you pipe. For large quantities of royal icing or butter cream, a nylon or plastic bag is preferable: a large greaseproof paper bag would be difficult to make and too awkward to handle.

Nozzles Choose good-quality nozzles free from dents or misshapen points and with a smooth, well-joined seam down the side. Piping nozzles are available in either metal or plastic. Metal ones are stronger and the tips are better moulded, giving a cleaner definition.

The kind of nozzle you use will depend on what icing you are doing. Choose the smaller sizes for fine or medium lettering or intricate piping with royal icing, and the larger ones – even a vegetable nozzle – for butter cream. Sizes can vary according to manufacturer, and you may have to try different makes to find

[continued overleaf]

MAKING A GREASEPROOF ICING BAG

1. Begin with a 25-cm/10-in square of greaseproof paper. Fold it in half diagonally to give a paper triangle of double thickness.
2. Curl the triangle round so that point A joins point B.
3. Take point C round the back to meet point A. Hold points A, B, C together, forming a cone making a point at D.

4. Secure the bag by folding points A, B, C over or stapling them all together. Snip off up to 1 cm/½ inch of the tip of the cone and slip in an icing nozzle from the top. You can even manage without a nozzle if you are using the bag for some of the less detailed kinds of icing, such as chocolate work: simply fill the finished bag with melted chocolate, snip off the very tip, and pipe as required.

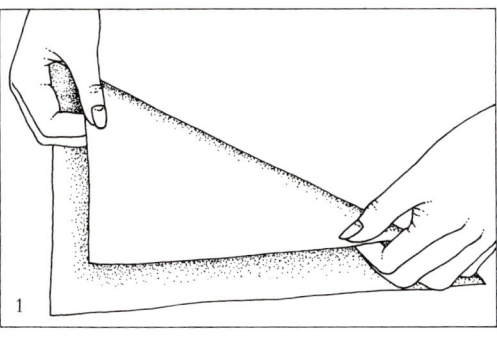

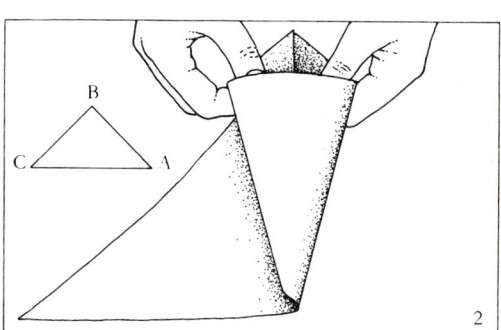

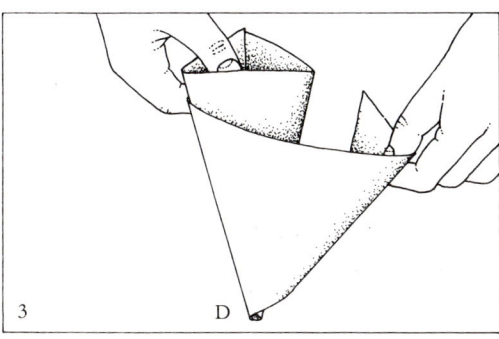

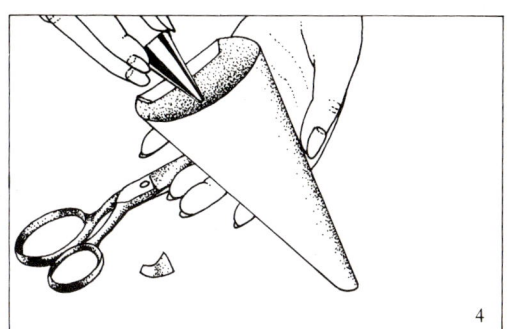

USEFUL EQUIPMENT

the nozzles that are most suitable. The most useful nozzles to begin with are illustrated here:

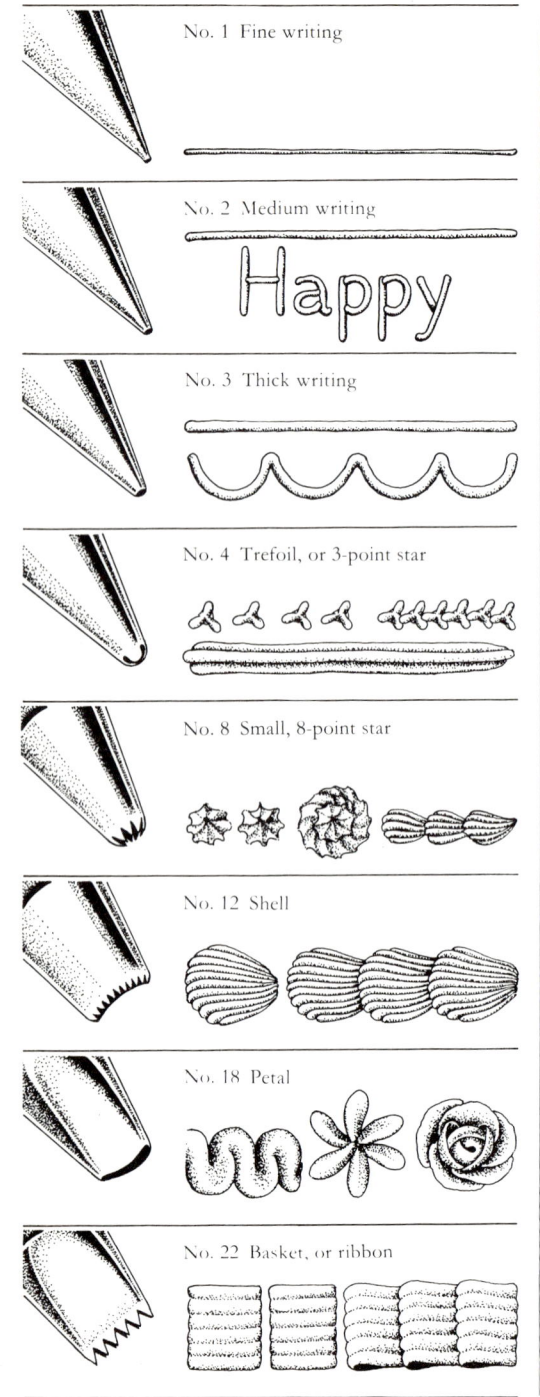

While the easiest way to identify the nozzle you want is by its number, you may find that some manufacturers number the same nozzle differently. The numbering for nozzles 1, 2 and 3 (fine, medium and thick writing) is fairly standard, but check when buying any other type that the number does correspond with the kind of nozzle you want.

Nozzles with a screw thread are designed to be attached from outside the icing bag to a connector fitted inside the bag and cannot be used with greaseproof paper bags. The idea of the connector is to allow you to change the nozzle without emptying the bag; simply unscrew one nozzle and screw on another. There are also connectors available for nozzles which don't have a screw thread, and these come in two parts: a screw fitting placed inside the icing bag and a collar which fits over the nozzle, holding it in place, and screws into the connector from outside.

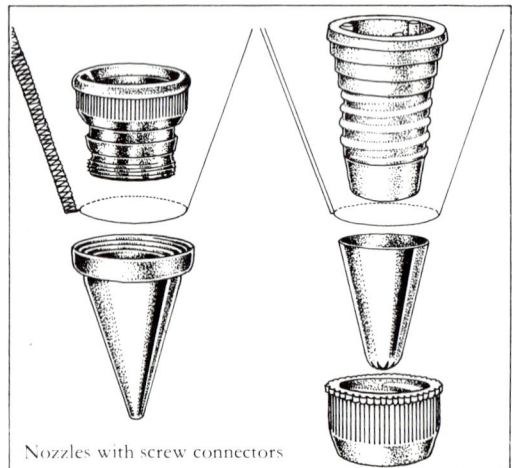

Nozzles with screw connectors

Icing syringes Often supplied as part of an icing set, the syringe consists of a large metal or plastic tube with a screw attachment for the nozzle at one end, containing a plunger with a ringed handle. Though it is easy to fill and simple to dismantle for cleaning, a syringe has its disadvantages. The plunger is more difficult to control than an icing bag since it does not have the same fingertip sensitivity to pressure, and air pockets can form, too, resulting in an uneven line of icing. It is also less comfortable to hold over a long period.

USEFUL EQUIPMENT

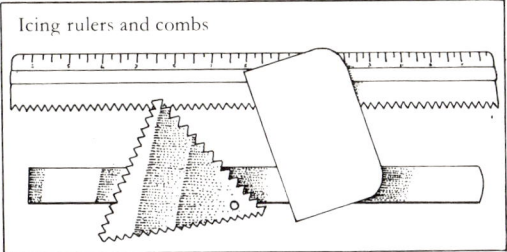
Icing rulers and combs

Icing ruler You need a straight edge for smoothing the icing on the cake when flat icing (applying the basic layers of royal icing before you start decorating). Use a metal or plastic icing ruler, which is like a conventional ruler but has no measurement markings, or has them on one side only – indentations would leave a trace on the surface. If the cake is not too large, you may be able to use a palette knife or the straight-edged back of a bread knife.

Icing comb This tool, made of plastic or metal and measuring about 13 × 7.5 cm/5 × 3 in, is for smoothing and decorating a cake. It is available with a straight or a serrated edge.

Icing nails If you are making flowers from royal icing, an icing nail is useful. It provides a rotatable surface on which each flower can be piped and consists of a small round piece of plastic or metal mounted on a long nail. To make a flower, fix a small square of waxed or greaseproof paper to the top with a blob of icing, then pipe with one hand while rotating the nail between the fingers and thumb of the other. Remove the paper and leave the flower to dry while you make the next one.

Icing moulds Also known as net nails, icing moulds are made of metal or plastic and are available in a variety of shapes. The moulds are supported on nails and used in a similar way to icing nails for piping raised designs such as trellis and basket work in royal icing. Instead of using paper, however, the surface of the mould is lightly greased and the piping applied to it and left to dry for 48 hours. You can then lift the design carefully off and arrange it on the cake.

It is possible to improvise icing moulds by using dariole moulds; or even upturned patty tins, lightly greased, for a shallow, curved decoration.

Templates or markers For a simple design you can make your own template. Just cut out a piece of card in the shape you want to follow and either pipe directly around it or mark the outline first with a series of pin pricks on the surface of the cake (see page 42). More complex designs can be created by using a piece of greaseproof paper the same size as the cake and drawing your pattern on it. Transfer this to the cake by making a series of pin pricks through the greaseproof paper to leave an outline on the top of the cake.

If you plan to ice many formal cakes, invest in some icing templates or markers. Made of metal

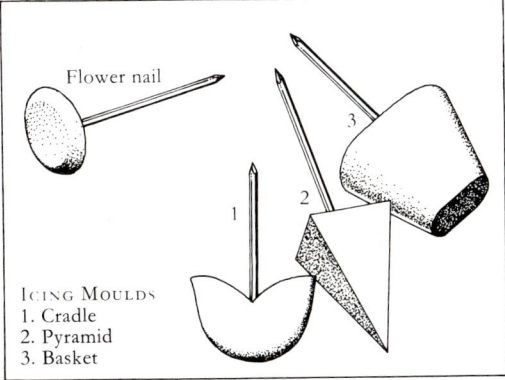
Flower nail

Icing Moulds
1. Cradle
2. Pyramid
3. Basket

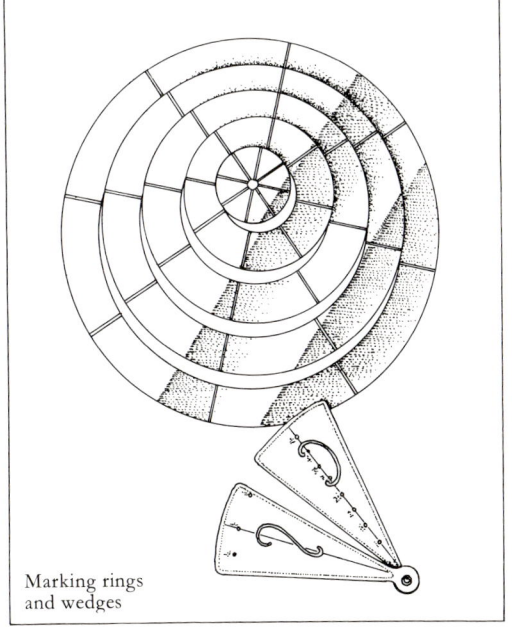
Marking rings and wedges

USEFUL EQUIPMENT

or plastic, these consist either of a set of different-sized rings marked in eighths, or in the shape of two flat triangular wedges attached at one corner to a pivotal pin on which the triangles swing to form symmetrical patterns on top of the cake.

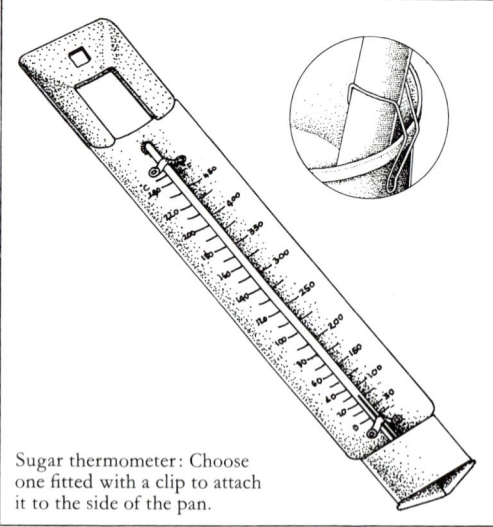

Sugar thermometer: Choose one fitted with a clip to attach it to the side of the pan.

Sugar thermometer If you are using icing such as boiled fondant and American frosting you will need a sugar thermometer to measure the exact temperature during boiling. This thermometer is specially designed to register the high temperatures of boiling sugar, and though one make may vary from another the range of degrees should be about 10–220 C/50–450 F. Choose a thermometer fitted with a clip to attach it to the side of the pan and prevent it from falling into the boiling liquid.

Never plunge a cold thermometer straight into a hot mixture or it may crack. Either stand it in a jug of warm water first or put it in the pan with the mixture from the beginning so that they heat up together. Similarly, always allow a hot thermometer to cool down gradually by transferring it from the pan to a jug or bowl of warm water.

ICING EXTRAS

These are a few additional items you may find helpful, though they are in no way essential.

A hat pin, easier to handle than an ordinary pin, is ideal for pricking round a template to mark out your design on the cake.

A small paint brush is useful for painting leaves and flowers with egg white when crystallising, and marzipan and fondant shapes with food colouring.

Tweezers enable you to handle delicate items such as fresh leaves and flowers without damaging them.

A dummy will allow you to practise icing techniques before trying them out on the cake itself. A polystyrene cake dummy covered with a permanent layer of basic flat icing can be used repeatedly for further practice. Otherwise you can use an upturned cake tin, but any metal ridge round the edge must be carefully iced to form a flat surface before you start.

CARE OF EQUIPMENT

When you've invested in good quality icing equipment, it's worth making it last as long as possible by proper cleaning and care.

To clean an icing nozzle after use, remove it from the piping bag and wash it in warm, soapy water. If some of the icing has set stubbornly hard, you may need to leave the nozzle to soak in the water for a few hours. Rinse and dry it thoroughly before storing.

Nylon or plastic icing bags are usually quite easy to wash out after use. Gently force out any surplus icing and wash the bag in warm, soapy water, turning it inside out. If the bag is particularly greasy or bears traces of food colouring, leave it to soak overnight in a bowl of warm water. Dry thoroughly before storing; the easiest way to dry icing bags inside and out is to invert them over an empty milk bottle or similar shape so that the moisture can drain out easily.

Icing syringes must be dismantled, washed in warm water, dried and stored carefully, especially if made of metal, as these are prone to rust.

Sugar thermometers should be cleaned immediately they have cooled after use. Use a soft brush and warm soapy water. If the thermometer is very sticky, it may be necessary to soak it first in hot water to soften the sugar. Dry thoroughly and store it in a damp-free place. Brass will tarnish and may develop verdigris, a poisonous blue-green coating, if exposed to moist conditions.

Cake Recipes

Although this book is about cake icing, it would not be complete unless we considered the basic cake underneath.

We judge its appeal by 'the icing on the cake', but whether it's a simple butter-iced sandwich or a more elaborate tiered confection, it would be more than a pity if the cake inside didn't live up to its presentation.

Here therefore is a selection of useful basic recipes for cakes that are suitable for a variety of different occasions. Some, like the lighter sponges and the genoese, are traditionally used with soft icings, such as butter cream and American or 7-minute frosting, since the creamy texture of these icings best matches the lightness of the cakes. If you want to ice a cake for a formal occasion – a wedding for instance – the more solid, long-keeping Rich fruit cake is the one to use, as this provides a good strong base for hard icings such as royal icing and kneaded fondant, and again, the firm textures of the cake, almond paste and icing go well together. Once dried out, royal icing also forms a lasting protective coating, which is invaluable on a cake that can keep for several months, even years.

A Victoria sandwich cake is a reliable standby for a quick birthday cake or special Sunday tea, but have you tried the all-in-one method for making a sandwich cake? This is so much quicker and easier, if time is short; do remember to use the soft tub margarine, though, as the recipe really does not work well with the hard, block types. When it comes to icing, however, stick to using soft butter cream or glacé icing, as this one-stage sandwich is slightly more crumbly in texture than the Victoria sandwich, making it difficult to spread frosting over the top.

Sandwich cakes should keep for 3–4 days if stored in an airtight tin. If you have a freezer, it's worth holding a batch of them ready there for emergencies. They will freeze for 2–3 months, don't take long to thaw, and with a few whirls of butter cream added – or frosting, and a chocolate curl or two – you have yourself a perfect tea-time treat.

A genoese sponge is the basis for many traditional gâteaux, as its lightness goes well with whipped cream and fruit fillings, for which the Victoria sandwich would be too heavy. It cuts easily, and will keep for 3–4 days in an airtight tin or for 2–3 months in the freezer. A simple whisked sponge can also make a delicious gâteau, but does not store so well and should really be eaten on the day it is made. That perennial favourite the Swiss roll makes a good standby, and it's surprisingly quick and easy to make once you get the knack.

Apart from the basic recipe for a Rich fruit cake, we have also given a Light fruit cake. This is a more economical cake, suitable for icing with lighter frostings, glacé icings and fondant as well as royal icing – the icing here being used in a purely decorative rather than protective way, since the cake itself is not designed to be as long-lasting as the Rich fruit cake. However, don't attempt to make a tiered cake with this lighter mixture as it is not firm enough to take the weight of each tier. The Farmhouse fruit cake, too, makes a pleasant alternative to rich cake and it has an unusual nutty, wholemeal flavour.

Finally, we haven't forgotten a favourite at children's parties – gingerbread, which you can decorate and make shapes from, or serve simply cut into slices.

A useful selection of standard cake tins would include the following:

One (450-g/1-lb) loaf tin
One (900-g/2-lb) loaf tin
One (33 × 23 cm/13 × 9 in) Swiss roll tin
Two (18-cm/7-in) round sandwich tins
One (18-cm/7-in) or (20-cm/8-in) square tin
One (18-cm/7-in) or (20-cm/8-in) round tin

PREPARING CAKE TINS

The richer the cake is, the more likely it is to stick to the tin during baking. You can avoid this by preparing the tin properly before filling it with the cake mixture. Begin by greasing the tin. For a whisked sponge, you need then only flour it; for a Victoria sandwich, you will need to line the base, while the richer genoese sponges and fruit cakes need tins that are completely lined. The lining paper must then also be greased, so that it peels away easily from the cooked cake.

Non-stick cake tins should not need either greasing or lining, but take care to follow the manufacturer's instructions when using these.

To line a round cake tin, begin by placing it upside down on greaseproof or non-stick paper and drawing round it to mark the size [1]. Cut out just inside the pencil line to leave a round of paper the same diameter as the tin.

Measure round the side of the tin with string. Cut one long strip of greaseproof or non-stick paper slightly longer than the piece of string to allow for overlap (or alternatively, two separate strips) and about 1 cm/½ in deeper than the tin. Fold up 1 cm/½ in all along one edge of the paper and cut slashes at an angle along this about 1 cm/½ in apart [2].

Lightly grease the inside of the tin with a pastry brush dipped in melted fat or oil. Fit the paper strips into the side of the tin [3]. Place the paper round in the bottom of the tin, covering the slashed edges [4]. Brush the paper with more melted fat or oil, unless you are using non-stick paper which will not need greasing.

To line a square cake tin, place the tin upside down on a square of greaseproof or non-stick paper at least 5 cm/2 in larger all round than the tin itself. Draw round the shape of the tin. Fold the paper along each side of the marked square, just inside the pencil lines. Using the fold as a guide, cut one side of each corner inwards as far as the outline of the tin [5].

Grease the inside of the tin with melted fat or oil. Fit the paper into the tin with the cut corners overlapping as shown [6]. Trim away any edges that stand above the top of the tin and brush the paper with melted fat or oil.

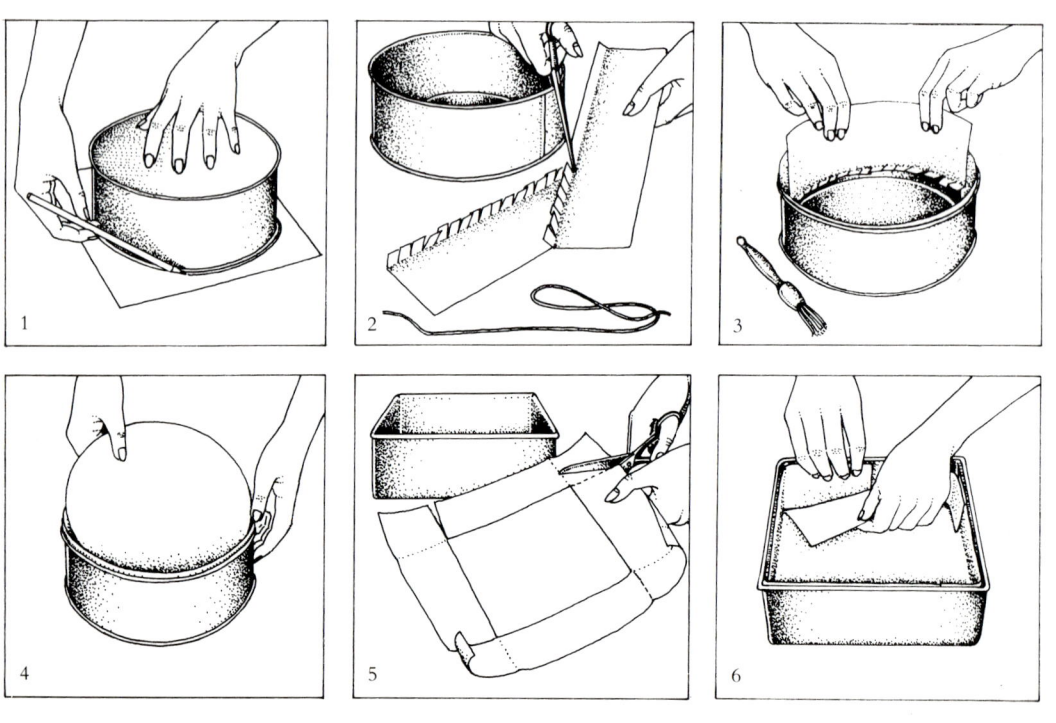

Basic Victoria sandwich

100 g/4 oz butter or block margarine
100 g/4 oz caster sugar
2 eggs
100 g/4 oz self-raising flour

Set the oven at moderate (160 C, 325 F, gas 3). Thoroughly grease and line the bases of two 18-cm (7-in) diameter round sandwich tins. Cream the fat until soft, then beat in the sugar; cream together until the mixture is light and fluffy. Beat the eggs together and add to the mixture a little at a time, beating thoroughly between each addition. Sift the flour and fold half of it in gently and evenly, using a metal spoon. Fold in the remaining flour in the same way.

Divide the mixture between the two tins and level the surface of each with a palette knife. Bake both the cakes on the same shelf in the centre of the oven for 25–30 minutes, until golden and firm to the touch and the mixture is beginning to shrink away from the sides of the tin.

Run a round-bladed knife around the edge to loosen the sides of the cakes from the tins, then quickly turn them out on to a wire rack to cool. Peel away the paper while the cakes are still hot. Fill the cakes as desired and sandwich together as directed in the recipes in Iced Cakes for all Occasions.

If you like the idea of a sandwich cake with a slightly caramelly flavour, use soft brown sugar instead of caster sugar. Don't use demerara sugar as the crystals are too large to dissolve evenly and will spoil the texture.

Basic one-stage sandwich

100 g/4 oz self-raising flour
1 teaspoon baking powder
100 g/4 oz soft tub margarine
100 g/4 oz caster sugar
2 eggs

Set the oven at moderate (170 C, 325 F, gas 3). Grease and line the bases of two 18-cm (7-in) diameter round sandwich tins. Sift together the flour and the baking powder and mix with the other ingredients. Beat hard with a wooden spoon for about 2 minutes, or for half the time with an electric beater.

Divide the mixture evenly between the two tins and level the surface. Bake both the cakes on the same shelf of the oven for about 25–30 minutes, until golden and firm to the touch, and the mixture is beginning to shrink away from the sides of the tin. Turn out on to a wire rack to cool. Spread one of the cakes with the desired filling (see Icings and Fillings) and sandwich together.

Flavourings for Basic Victoria and One-stage sandwich cakes

Orange or lemon Lightly fold the finely grated rind and 1 tablespoon of the juice of an orange or lemon into the finished mixture.

Chocolate Replace 3 tablespoons flour with an equal amount of cocoa powder.

Coffee For the Victoria sandwich, add 2 teaspoons instant coffee powder dissolved in ½ teaspoon warm water to the finished mixture. For the One-stage sandwich, mix the dissolved coffee in with all the other ingredients.

Nut Add 25 g/1 oz chopped walnuts, hazelnuts or almonds to the completed mixture for both cakes.

Spice Sift the flour with 1½ teaspoons ground mixed spice before adding to either mixture.

Basic whisked sponge

3 large eggs
100 g/4 oz caster sugar
75 g/3 oz plain flour

Set the oven at moderately hot (190 C, 375 F, gas 5). Grease two 18-cm (7-in) diameter round sandwich tins and lightly dust with flour, shaking off the excess.

In a large bowl, whisk the eggs and sugar over a pan of hot water until the mixture is thick and pale. Use a hand-held electric whisk if you can, as the mixture will need a good deal of whisking. To test if the correct thickness has been reached, lift the whisk and let the mixture drip off into the bowl in a particular shape – a 'W' for instance – as shown. If the 'W' holds its shape for a few seconds before dissolving into the rest of the mixture you will know that the mixture is ready.

Remove the bowl from the heat and continue whisking until cool. Lightly fold in the flour with a metal spoon. Divide the mixture between the tins and bake for 20–25 minutes until golden and firm to the touch. Turn out and cool on a wire rack.

When cool, the cakes may be sandwiched together with jam, butter cream or whipped fresh cream and fruit.

Whisk until you can leave a ribbon trail in the mixture.

Genoese sponge

A genoese sponge is the starting point for innumerable classical gâteaux, sandwiched with rich, luxurious fillings like butter cream, crème au beurre, whipped fresh cream and fruit purée. It is also traditionally the sponge to use when making little cakes, topped with almond paste, glacé icing or fondant – Iced fancies (see page 105) is a good example.

The main things to bear in mind when making genoese are that the eggs and sugar have to be whisked to exactly the right consistency, and the flour and butter folded in as lightly as possible.

40 g/1½ oz unsalted butter
65 g/2½ oz plain flour
1 tablespoon cornflour
3 large eggs
75 g/3 oz caster sugar

Set the oven at moderately hot (190 C, 375 F gas 5). Line and grease two round 18-cm (7-in) diameter sandwich tins. Melt the butter very gently and allow to cool for a few minutes. Meanwhile sift together the flour and cornflour.

Whisk the eggs and sugar in a large bowl over a pan of hot water until light and creamy and the whisk, when lifted, leaves a ribbon trail for a few seconds in the mixture. Then remove the bowl from the heat and continue whisking until cool. Fold in half the flour using a metal spoon. Pour the butter around the inside of the bowl while folding in the remaining flour as quickly as possible, as the sponge will soon lose volume after the butter is added.

Divide the mixture evenly between the tins and bake for 20–25 minutes until golden and firm to the touch. Turn out and cool on a wire rack. Sandwich together when cool with any of the fillings suggested above and decorate as desired.

Swiss roll

3 large eggs
100 g/4 oz caster sugar
100 g/4 oz plain flour
1 tablespoon hot water
caster sugar for dredging

Set the oven at hot (220 C, 425 F, gas 7). Grease and line a 33 × 23 cm (13 × 9 in) Swiss roll tin. In a large bowl, whisk the eggs and sugar over a pan of hot water until the mixture is thick and pale. It should be thick enough to hold its shape for a few seconds when you lift the whisk. Remove from the heat and continue whisking until cool. Sift the flour and gently fold in half of it with a metal spoon, then fold in the remainder together with the hot water. When evenly mixed, turn the mixture into the lined tin, spreading it over the whole of the base. Bake for about 8 minutes or until golden and firm to the touch.

Meanwhile, place a damp tea towel on the worktop and cover this with a sheet of greaseproof paper. Sprinkle with caster sugar. When the Swiss roll is cooked, quickly turn it out on to the sugared paper and peel off the lining paper. Trim crusty edges from the cake with a sharp knife. Using the tea towel as a guide, roll up the sponge from the short end with the greaseproof paper inside.

When completely cool, the Swiss roll can be unrolled, spread with jam, butter cream or whipped fresh cream, then rolled up again.

If preferred, the Swiss roll can be filled with jam while warm and rolled up using the greaseproof paper as a guide. Always allow the cake to cool though before filling with butter cream or fresh cream.

Chocolate Swiss roll Replace 1 tablespoon of the flour with an equal amount of cocoa powder. Fill with Chocolate butter cream (see page 28).

1. Peel away the lining paper quickly before the cake cools.

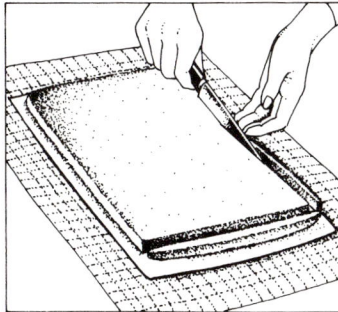

2. Trim with a sharp knife to give clean-cut edges.

3. Roll the sponge and greaseproof paper together and leave to cool.

Light fruit cake

This is a popular cake for a family tea which you can serve either as it is or iced with glacé icing, royal icing, frosting or fondant, depending on the occasion. It's very good for a birthday or Christmas if you're looking for a lighter alternative to the Rich fruit cake. Although not so long-keeping as the Rich fruit cake, it will mature well if you store it for 4–5 days in an airtight tin before cutting it.

200 g/7 oz butter or block margarine
200 g/7 oz soft light brown sugar
3 large eggs
175 g/6 oz plain flour
175 g/6 oz self-raising flour
50 g/2 oz glacé cherries, halved
275 g/10 oz mixed dried fruit
3 tablespoons milk

Set the oven at moderate (170 C, 325 F, gas 3). Grease and line a 20-cm (8-in) diameter round or 18-cm (7-in) square cake tin. Cream the butter or margarine until soft, beat in the sugar and continue to cream until the mixture is light and fluffy. Gradually beat in the eggs a little at a time. Sift together the flours and fold half into the mixture with the cherries. Fold in the remaining flour and the dried fruit, mixing in the milk to soften the mixture.

Turn the mixture into the tin, level the surface and bake for about 1 hour 25 minutes or until firm and golden and a skewer inserted into the centre of the cake comes out clean. Cool for a few minutes in the tin. Turn the cake out and finish cooling it on a wire rack.

Rich fruit cake

A Rich fruit cake is the classic cake for all formal occasions – 18th birthdays, engagements, weddings, anniversaries – as well as the traditional favourite for Christmas. The main thing to remember when making it is that this is not a cake you can bake one day and eat the next; it has to mature for at least a month to allow the rum or brandy to soak in and the juices from all the dried fruit to moisten it, and the characteristic rich, dark colour to develop. If you cut it too soon, you may find it disappointingly dry and crumbly.

For basic quantities see opposite

Set the oven at cool (150 C, 300 F, gas 2). Prepare the cake tin by thoroughly greasing and lining it. Tie a double thickness of brown paper or newspaper firmly round the outside of the tin to prevent the outside edges of the cake from cooking too quickly. Wash the dried fruit (unless you are using pre-washed fruit) and glacé cherries, drain well and dry thoroughly by wrapping them in a clean tea towel. Mix together the fruit, nuts, chopped peel and finely grated lemon rind. Sift the flour with the mixed spice. Cream the butter with the sugar until light and fluffy, then gradually beat in the eggs. Fold in the flour alternately with the fruit and nuts until evenly mixed. Stir in the brandy or rum. Spoon into the prepared tin and bake for the time indicated on the chart, reducing the temperature halfway through to 140 C (275 F, gas 1).

Cook until evenly risen, golden brown and firm. A skewer inserted into the centre should come out clean and the cake should be just beginning to shrink away from the sides of the tin. Cool in the tin for about an hour, then turn out and allow to finish cooling on a wire rack. When cool, you can prick all over the base of the cake with a skewer and spoon a few tablespoons of brandy or rum, if liked, over the surface to keep the cake moist during storage.

To store, wrap the cake tightly in a double thickness of greaseproof paper followed by kitchen foil and leave in a cool, dry place to mature for at least one month.

CAKE RECIPES

Ingredient quantities for Rich fruit cakes

Round tin: Square tin:	15 cm/6 in 13 cm/5 in	18 cm/7 in 15 cm/6 in	20 cm/8 in 18 cm/7 in	23 cm/9 in 20 cm/8 in
Raisins	50 g/2 oz	75 g/3 oz	100 g/4 oz	150 g/5 oz
Sultanas	50 g/2 oz	75 g/3 oz	150 g/5 oz	200 g/7 oz
Currants	175 g/6 oz	225 g/8 oz	275 g/10 oz	375 g/13 oz
Glacé cherries	50 g/2 oz	65 g/2½ oz	75 g/3 oz	100 g/4 oz
Chopped nuts	40 g/1½ oz	50 g/2 oz	75 g/3 oz	100 g/4 oz
Mixed peel	40 g/1½ oz	50 g/2 oz	75 g/3 oz	100 g/4 oz
Lemon rind	½ teaspoon	1 teaspoon	1½ teaspoons	2 teaspoons
Plain flour	100 g/4 oz	150 g/5 oz	200 g/7 oz	250 g/9 oz
Mixed spice	½ teaspoon	1 teaspoon	1½ teaspoons	2 teaspoons
Butter, softened	75 g/3 oz	100 g/4 oz	175 g/6 oz	225 g/8 oz
Soft brown sugar	75 g/3 oz	100 g/4 oz	175 g/6 oz	225 g/8 oz
Eggs	2	3	4	5
Brandy or rum	1 tablespoon	1½ tablespoons	2 tablespoons	2½ tablespoons
Cooking time	1¾–2 hrs (approx)	2–2¼ hrs	2¼–2½ hrs	2½–3 hrs

Ingredient quantities (continued)

Round tin: Square tin:	25 cm/10 in 23 cm/9 in	28 cm/11 in 25 cm/10 in	30 cm/12 in 28 cm/11 in	33 cm/13 in 30 cm/12 in
Raisins	175 g/6 oz	200 g/7 oz	225 g/8 oz	250 g/9 oz
Sultanas	225 g/8 oz	350 g/12 oz	375 g/13 oz	450 g/1 lb
Currants	500 g/1 lb 2 oz	550 g/1 lb 4 oz	675 g/1 lb 8 oz	800 g/1 lb 12 oz
Glacé cherries	125 g/4½ oz	175 g/6 oz	200 g/7 oz	225 g/8 oz
Chopped nuts	125 g/4½ oz	175 g/6 oz	200 g/7 oz	225 g/8 oz
Mixed peel	125 g/4½ oz	175 g/6 oz	200 g/7 oz	225 g/8 oz
Lemon rind	2½ teaspoons	3 teaspoons	3½ teaspoons	4 teaspoons
Plain flour	300 g/11 oz	400 g/14 oz	450 g/1 lb	500 g/1 lb 2 oz
Mixed spice	2¼ teaspoons	2½ teaspoons	3½ teaspoons	4 teaspoons
Butter, softened	250 g/9 oz	350 g/12 oz	400 g/14 oz	450 g/1 lb
Soft brown sugar	250 g/9 oz	350 g/12 oz	400 g/14 oz	450 g/1 lb
Eggs	7	8	10	12
Brandy or rum	3½ tablespoons	4 tablespoons	5 tablespoons	6 tablespoons
Cooking time	2¾–3¼ hrs (approx)	3–3½ hrs	3¼–3¾ hrs	3¾–4¼ hrs

Farmhouse fruit cake

100 g/4 oz raisins
100 g/4 oz currants
100 g/4 oz sultanas
50 g/2 oz chopped mixed peel
50 g/2 oz walnuts
15 g/½ oz sesame seeds
225 g/8 oz wholemeal flour
2 teaspoons baking powder
1 teaspoon mixed spice
225 g/8 oz butter
225 g/8 oz Muscovado or soft dark brown sugar
4 eggs

Set the oven at moderate (170 C, 325 F, gas 3). Grease and line a 23-cm (9-in) diameter round or 20-cm (8-in) square cake tin. Wash the fruit (if it has not been already), drain and dry well. Chop the walnuts roughly and mix with the fruit and sesame seeds. Sift together the flour, baking powder and spice and stir in any bran left in the sieve. Cream the butter until soft, mix in the sugar and beat thoroughly until the mixture is smooth and lighter in colour. Add the eggs a little at a time, beating well between each addition. Fold in the flour and fruit alternately until evenly mixed.

Turn the mixture into the prepared tin and level the top. Bake for 1 hour 50 minutes to 2 hours until firm and a skewer inserted into the centre comes out clean. Cool slightly in the tin, then turn out and allow to finish cooling on a wire rack.

Gingerbread

675 g/1½ lb plain flour
2 teaspoons baking powder
1 tablespoon mixed spice
½ teaspoon cinnamon
2 teaspoons ginger
pinch of salt
8 tablespoons golden syrup
275 g/10 oz soft brown sugar
50 g/2 oz butter or block margarine
finely grated rind and juice of ½ a lemon
1 egg
1 egg yolk

Set the oven at moderate (170 C, 325 F, gas 3). Grease and flour two 33 × 23 cm (13 × 9 in) Swiss roll tins. Sift together the flour, baking powder and spices with the salt. Gently heat the syrup, sugar and butter or margarine together in a pan until thoroughly dissolved. Add the lemon rind and juice and allow to cool slightly. Make a well in the centre of the flour mixture and pour in the syrup mixture; beat thoroughly to mix, then add the eggs, kneading until smooth.

Roll the gingerbread out on a floured surface to fit the tins. Lift it carefully into the tins, pressing the mixture well into the corners. Bake for about 35 minutes until firm to the touch. Cool for 1 minute in the tins, then run a knife around the inside of each and turn the gingerbread out.

Cut it into the required shapes while it is still warm and leave to cool on a wire rack.

For gingerbread men, the shapes can be cut from the rolled-out dough before baking, then lifted on to greased baking sheets for cooking.

Note If you only have one Swiss roll tin bake the gingerbread in two batches.

Icings and Fillings

Now to the icing; its choice and treatment will play a vital role in the success of your efforts and the effect of the final creation.

Icings vary tremendously in type from fluffy, soft-textured buttery mixtures to the hard, white, formal royal icing used for more elaborate cakes. Your choice of icing and filling – if used – should depend upon the cake you are icing, the occasion it's for and the kind of effect you're after.

The softer types of icing can also be used as fillings. Butter cream and its richer cousin, crème au beurre, both make excellent spreadable fillings and toppings for sponge cakes. Others, like glacé, fondant and royal icing, are really more suitable as smooth and decorative exterior coatings. Generally, more formal cakes use the harder icings, royal and fondant, largely because of the smooth, classic effects they can create. In addition, royal icing has excellent keeping qualities. Since it can be completely dried out, royal icing on a cake will keep for months, even years if stored correctly: a rich fruit cake with royal icing should be wrapped in double layers of greaseproof paper, then in kitchen foil, and stored in a cardboard box in a cool, dry place. The cake will mature well and go on improving for up to a year, remaining quite edible several years later. You may well find, however, that the icing has discoloured as a result of oils gradually seeping through from the almond paste underneath. This almost inevitably happens during long storage: all you need do is remove the existing layers of icing and re-ice the cake before you use it.

Many icings have the advantage of starting out pure white in colour. This not only looks very impressive as it is, it also enables the icing to take other colours particularly well. What colours you choose depends very much upon the occasion: white is the obvious choice for weddings and many other formal occasions, but delicate pinks and blues are often used for christening cakes, yellow for golden wedding celebrations and so on. Most people prefer pale pastel colours, so as a rule it is safer to keep your colours delicate unless a special effect is needed. Bright holly green and berry red, for instance, are useful colourings for Christmas cakes, as long as you buy the correct ones: there are a great many different reds and greens but you need the right ones for a seasonal effect.

Food colourings are available either in liquid or paste form. When you're adding colouring to an icing, add it very carefully, a little at a time, as usually only a small amount is required. The safest way to do this with liquid colouring is to dip a skewer briefly into the bottle and allow the colouring to drip off into the icing; beat this in until well mixed. Continue in this way until you have achieved the shade you want. You may find from experience that some colourings, especially the paste variety, actually darken as the icing dries out, so you may need to allow for this initially.

Choose your icing to match your cake, both in texture and flavour; soft, fluffy icings on the lighter sponges, and heavier, harder icings on rich fruit cakes. You can colour and flavour an icing or filling to match the cake or to contrast with it: lemon icing on a coffee-flavoured cake, for instance, is a popular combination. With confidence, you'll learn to mix and match and discover the tremendous variety open to you.

Butter icing or butter cream

This is one of the most useful of the basic icings as it can be used for coating or filling, piping or spreading, and can be flavoured or coloured as desired. When applied to the sides of a cake it can hold additional decorations like chopped nuts and desiccated coconut (see page 38). You can use it on any type of cake that's going to be eaten fresh, or you can freeze it.

The quantity given here will fill and coat the top and sides of a 20-cm/8-in sandwich cake. More will be needed for piping decorations on the top. And if you want the icing to be firmer, simply increase the amount of icing sugar slightly.

100 g/4 oz unsalted butter or margarine
225 g/8 oz icing sugar
1–2 tablespoons milk
flavouring (see below)

Beat the butter or margarine until soft. Gradually beat in the icing sugar. Add the milk and chosen flavouring and beat thoroughly until smooth.

VARIATIONS

Orange or lemon Substitute fresh orange or lemon juice for the milk.
Coffee Replace the milk with 1 tablespoon instant coffee dissolved in 1 tablespoon hot water.
Chocolate Replace 1 tablespoon of the milk with 1 tablespoon cocoa powder dissolved in 2 tablespoons hot water.
Liqueur Any liqueur can be used in place of the milk.
Vanilla Crush half a vanilla pod and infuse it in the milk for about an hour. Then strain the milk and use as instructed above.

Alternatively, you can add a few drops of vanilla essence to the butter cream.

Crème au beurre

This is a rich and glossy soft icing, buttery and luxurious, ideal for special gâteaux. You will need a sugar-boiling thermometer to make it successfully.

This quantity is enough to fill and top an 18-cm/7-in round cake or a 15-cm/6-in square one.

75 g/3 oz granulated or caster sugar
4 tablespoons water
2 egg yolks
175 g/6 oz unsalted butter

Put the sugar and water in a heavy-based pan and dissolve over a gentle heat, stirring occasionally, without allowing the mixture to boil. Once the sugar has dissolved, bring to a rapid boil and boil without stirring for 2–3 minutes until the temperature reaches 107 C/225 F on a sugar thermometer. Beat the egg yolks lightly in a bowl and pour the hot syrup into them in a thin, steady stream, whisking hard all the time. Continue whisking until the mixture is thick and cold. Cream the butter until soft and beat into the mixture.

VARIATIONS

Beat in any of the following with the butter:
Chocolate 50 g/2 oz melted dessert chocolate.
Coffee 1 tablespoon coffee essence.
Orange or lemon 1 teaspoon juice and finely grated rind to taste.
Liqueur 1 tablespoon of any liqueur.
Fruit 50–100 g/2–4 oz fruit purée from fruits such as fresh strawberries, raspberries and cooked apricots. Pass the fruit through a sieve or blend it in a liquidiser to make the purée.

Glacé icing

Glacé icing is perhaps the most basic of all icings, and the simplest to make. It is mainly used for icing the tops of sponge cakes, either plain or feather-iced (see page 37). It can be coloured, using the standard food colourings, or varied as desired with coffee, orange juice and other flavours. If you are adding liquid flavourings, omit an equal quantity of water or the icing will be too thin.

This quantity will cover the top of a 20-cm/8-in round or an 18-cm/7-in square cake.

225 g/8 oz icing sugar
2–3 tablespoons warm water

Sift the icing sugar into a mixing bowl and gradually stir in enough water to make a smooth consistency; the icing should be thick enough to coat the back of a wooden spoon. If you do accidentally make it the wrong consistency though, don't worry: just beat in a little more sifted icing sugar or warm water as necessary. Use immediately or transfer it to an airtight container to prevent a crust forming. If you store the container in a refrigerator the icing will keep for several days, needing only a little beating to be ready for use.

VARIATIONS

Orange or lemon Substitute strained fresh orange or lemon juice for the water.
Coffee Dissolve 1 tablespoon instant coffee in the measured water.
Chocolate Dissolve 1 tablespoon cocoa powder in the measured water.
Liqueur Any liqueur can be used in place of the measured water.

Fudge icing

This makes a popular filling and topping for less formal cakes. It can be swirled, forked into a design or 'peaked' like rough icing (see page 41). It sets firmly on the cake while remaining soft-textured to eat.

This quantity will fill and ice the top and sides of a 20-cm/8-in round or an 18-cm/7-in square cake.

75 g/3 oz unsalted butter or margarine
3 tablespoons milk or cream
350 g/12 oz icing sugar, sifted

Put all the ingredients into a mixing bowl over a pan of hot water. Stir well until the mixture is smooth and glossy. Remove the bowl from the heat and beat hard until the mixture begins to thicken. As soon as the icing is thick enough to hold its shape, while still remaining spreadable, apply it to the cake using a palette knife.

VARIATIONS

Chocolate Dissolve 1 tablespoon cocoa powder in 2 tablespoons hot water and use to replace 2 tablespoons of the milk.
Lemon or orange Use 2 tablespoons orange or lemon juice to replace the same amount of milk, plus a little finely grated rind to taste.
Coffee Dissolve 1 tablespoon instant coffee in 1 tablespoon very hot water and use to replace the same amount of milk.
Caramel Substitute soft brown sugar for the icing sugar.

American frosting

This is a fluffy, light-textured icing which holds its shape well and is usually used to coat sponge cakes. It will keep on a cake for slightly longer than the butter-based icings, remaining good to eat for up to a week. You will need a sugar-boiling thermometer to make it as the temperature of the sugar syrup is critical to the success of the frosting.

This amount will cover the top and sides of an 18-cm/7-in round cake or a 15-cm/6-in square one.

225 g/8 oz granulated or caster sugar
4 tablespoons water
pinch of cream of tartar
1 egg white

Put the sugar and water into a small pan. Add the cream of tartar and stir over a gentle heat, without allowing the mixture to boil, until the sugar has completely dissolved. Then bring to the boil, without stirring, and boil rapidly until the temperature reaches 120 C/240 F on a sugar thermometer. Whisk the egg white until stiff and pour the boiling sugar syrup into it, whisking hard. Continue to whisk until the mixture begins to thicken and dull slightly. Quickly turn it out on to the cake and spread it evenly with a palette knife.

VARIATIONS

Coffee After adding the sugar syrup, whisk in 1 teaspoon coffee essence.
Lemon or orange After adding the sugar syrup, whisk in 1 teaspoon lemon or orange juice and a little finely grated rind to taste.
Caramel Substitute demerara or soft dark brown sugar for white sugar.

7-minute frosting

This is a simpler alternative to American frosting which does not require the use of a sugar thermometer. It will not set as firmly though and should be eaten within 24 hours.

This amount will cover the top and sides of a 20-cm (8-in) round cake or an 18-cm (7-in) square one.

1 egg white
175 g/6 oz caster sugar
2 tablespoons hot water
pinch each of cream of tartar and salt

Put all the ingredients into a bowl over a pan of hot water. Whisk until the mixture thickens and forms soft peaks – this should take about 7 minutes with an electric hand whisk or twice as long with a simple manual one. Remove the bowl from the heat and turn the frosting out on to the cake, spreading it with a palette knife.

The same variations in flavouring that are used with American frosting can be used here. Add the flavourings at the beginning with all the other ingredients.

Apricot glaze

Apricot glaze is used mainly to attach almond paste firmly to the surface of a rich fruit cake, but you can also brush it on top of a cake as a decorative glaze. This quantity will cover the top and sides of four 20-cm (8-in) round cakes.

Redcurrant jam can be used as a variation.

225 g/8 oz apricot jam
2 tablespoons water
2 teaspoons lemon juice

Warm the jam gently in the water until melted, then rub it through a fine nylon sieve. Add the lemon juice and apply the glaze while still warm to the surface of the cake with a pastry brush, as directed in each recipe.

Pour left-over glaze into a screw-topped jar. It will keep in the refrigerator for several weeks.

Almond paste

Almond paste is perhaps most familiar to us as the base layer under royal icing on formal wedding or Christmas cakes. It gives a smooth surface for the icing and protects it from discoloration as well as contributing to the taste and texture of the whole cake. It has many other uses, however, as it takes colour well and can easily be moulded (see pages 47–48).

If well wrapped in cling-film or cooking foil, almond paste will keep moist in the refrigerator for about a month, or it can be frozen for up to three months. You may find it easier to make a larger quantity at a time than you need; the remainder can either be stored in this way or modelled into animals and other decorations for your cake.

Makes 900 g/2 lb

225 g/8 oz icing sugar
225 g/8 oz caster sugar
450 g/1 lb ground almonds
4 egg yolks, or 2 whole eggs
a few drops almond essence
1 teaspoon lemon juice

Sift the icing sugar and mix in a large bowl with the caster sugar and ground almonds. Beat the eggs lightly with the almond essence and lemon juice. Make a well in the middle of the ground almond mixture and stir in the eggs. Mix, gradually drawing in the almond mixture until all the ingredients bind together to make a firm paste. Store until needed in an airtight container or polythene wrap to prevent the paste from drying out.

Economical almond paste

This is an economical version of almond paste which cuts down on the most expensive ingredient – the almonds. It won't keep on a cake for as long as the real thing, but it should remain good for several weeks.

Makes about 900 g/2 lb

275 g/10 oz granulated sugar
250 ml/8 fl oz water
225 g/8 oz butter or margarine
175 g/6 oz fine semolina
175 g/6 oz ground almonds
1 teaspoon almond essence
1 teaspoon vanilla essence

Bring the sugar and water to the boil together and boil the mixture over a medium heat for about 5 minutes until it is thick and syrupy, but has not yet begun to turn brown. Remove the pan from the heat.

In a separate pan, melt the butter or margarine, stir in the semolina and brown lightly. Add the ground almonds and the almond and vanilla essences to taste. Transfer this mixture to the pan containing the syrup and reheat gently, stirring continuously, until well-mixed and thick. Leave the paste to cook gently for 3 minutes.

Take the pan from the heat and allow the paste to cool. Use it immediately or store it in an airtight container to prevent it from drying out.

Quantities required to cover both top and sides of standard cakes	Round	Quantity	Square	Quantity
	15 cm/6 in	350 g/12 oz	13 cm/5 in	350 g/12 oz
	18 cm/7 in	450 g/1 lb	15 cm/6 in	450 g/1 lb
	20 cm/8 in	675 g/1½ lb	18 cm/7 in	675 g/1½ lb
	23 cm/9 in	900 g/2 lb	20 cm/8 in	900 g/2 lb
	25 cm/10 in	1.25 kg/2½ lb	23 cm/9 in	1.25 kg/2½ lb
	28 cm/11 in	1.4 kg/3 lb	25 cm/10 in	1.4 kg/3 lb
	30 cm/12 in	1.5 kg/3½ lb	28 cm/11 in	1.5 kg/3½ lb
	33 cm/13 in	1.8 kg/4 lb	30 cm/12 in	1.8 kg/4 lb

Royal icing

Royal icing is most commonly used to make formal designs on cakes for special celebrations like weddings or Christmas. It dries to a hard white finish and with practice you can achieve a perfectly smooth surface. You can spread it smooth as in flat icing, rough it up into peaks, or pipe it into intricate designs.

The glycerine in this recipe helps to keep the icing from becoming too hard on a long-keeping cake. When icing the lower tiers of a wedding cake though, you should quarter the quantity of glycerine given below, or the icing may be too soft to take the weight of the tiers above. For a really bright, white appearance, a very little blue food colouring may be added to the icing. Albumen powder can be used as a substitute for egg whites and this means you do not have the problem of left-over egg yolks.

4 egg whites or 25 g/1 oz albumen powder
900 g/2 lb icing sugar, sifted
1 tablespoon lemon juice (optional)
2 teaspoons glycerine

Lightly beat the egg whites with a fork. If you are using albumen powder, dissolve this in 175 ml/6 fl oz cold water and leave to stand for 1 hour, stirring occasionally. Transfer the egg white or albumen to a large mixing bowl and gradually begin to stir in the icing sugar, beating with a wooden spoon or electric mixer. Add the lemon juice and glycerine if desired. Beat thoroughly until smooth, continuing to add icing sugar until the correct consistency is obtained. For flat icing, the icing should hold soft peaks when lifted on the whisk but they should fall slowly. For rough icing and decorative piping it should pull up into firm peaks which hold their shape. For piping lines the icing should be somewhere between the two in consistency.

As soon as the icing is made, cover it with a damp cloth or transfer it to an airtight container to prevent a crust forming before you have managed to use it. Covered with a damp cloth, the icing will keep moist for up to 24 hours; in an airtight container, it will keep for a week. You can therefore make a large quantity at a time. This is particularly useful for flat icing, when each layer has to dry out for 24 hours before the next can be applied.

	Round	Quantity	Square	Quantity
Quantities required to cover formal cakes (450 g/1 lb icing sugar makes 450 g/1 lb Royal icing)	15 cm/6 in	450 g/1 lb	13 cm/5 in	450 g/1 lb
	18 cm/7 in	575 g/1¼ lb	15 cm/6 in	575 g/1¼ lb
	20 cm/8 in	675 g/1½ lb	18 cm/7 in	675 g/1½ lb
	23 cm/9 in	900 g/2 lb	20 cm/8 in	900 g/2 lb
	25 cm/10 in	1 kg/2¼ lb	23 cm/9 in	1 kg/2¼ lb
	28 cm/11 in	1.25 kg/2½ lb	25 cm/10 in	1.25 kg/2½ lb
	30 cm/12 in	1.4 kg/3 lb	28 cm/11 in	1.4 kg/3 lb
	33 cm/13 in	1.6 kg/3½ lb	30 cm/12 in	1.6 kg/3½ lb

Boiled fondant icing

Fondant icing gives a smooth, even coating to cakes of all sizes. Boiled fondant is widely used commercially, as it can be produced in large quantities and easily stored; if placed in its dry form in a sealed container it will keep for two or three months, ready to be moulded or warmed to a pouring consistency with stock syrup.

You will need a sugar thermometer for making this type of fondant, as the temperature is critical; underheated fondant will not set well and if overheated, it will become hard and dull. It is made from sugar and water boiled together, with cream of tartar or glucose added to prevent the texture from becoming granular, like fudge.

675 g/1½ lb granulated sugar
300 ml/½ pint water
1½ tablespoons liquid glucose or ¼ teaspoon cream of tartar

Place the sugar and water in a clean pan and heat very gently, without stirring, until the sugar has completely dissolved. (Stirring may cause the sugar to crystallise.) Then add the glucose or cream of tartar. Place the sugar thermometer in the pan and slowly bring the mixture to the boil. Boil rapidly, without stirring, until the temperature reaches 115 C/240 F, occasionally brushing the sides of the pan with a pastry brush dipped in hot water to prevent sugar crystals forming. (If one or two crystals form, the rest of the mixture will very quickly follow suit.)

Immediately the temperature is reached, remove the pan from the heat and, if you want the fondant to be of a pouring consistency, transfer it to a large, chilled, wetted earthenware mixing bowl. Beat the mixture hard as it cools. It will gradually become white and opaque and once it has cooled down to 27–30 C/80–85 F (check with the sugar thermometer) it is ready for pouring over the cake. This is also the moment to add a few drops of food colouring, if liked.

To make the fondant of a mouldable consistency, as soon as it has reached the temperature of 115 C/240 F pour it straight from the pan on to a cold, wetted marble slab or into a large, chilled, wetted mixing bowl as before [1]. Begin to work the fondant as you pour it, using a wooden spatula or a metal palette knife [2], lifting the mixture with smooth strokes from the outside to the middle and working round until it changes from a clear liquid to a creamy paste. Now knead in a few drops of food colouring, if liked. Continue working the fondant with your hands as it thickens – it will get progressively harder to work as it firms up – until it finally becomes a solid white mass [3]. (If you are making the fondant in a mixing bowl you may find it easier to beat it well with a wooden spoon rather than work it with palette knife and hands.) You can now mould the fondant or cut it into shapes as directed in each recipe, or alternatively you can shape it into small balls and place them in a screw-topped jar for storage.

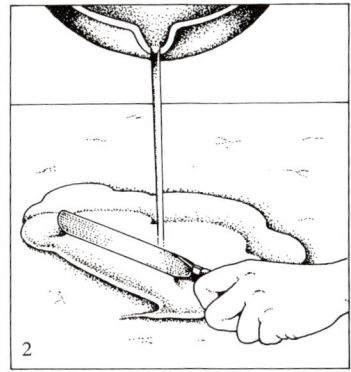
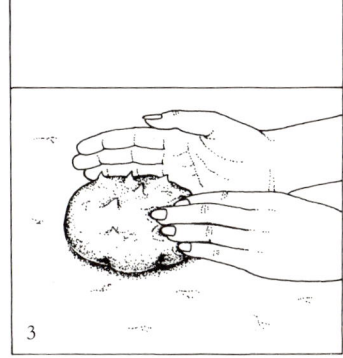

Stock syrup

FOR BOILED FONDANT

450 g/1 lb granulated sugar
450 ml/¾ pint water

Place the sugar and water in a clean pan and allow to dissolve over a gentle heat without stirring, as for boiled fondant. Bring to the boil, take the pan off the heat and leave the syrup to cool slightly. Store it in a screw-topped jar.

TO USE BOILED FONDANT
AFTER STORING

Boiled fondant can be moulded almost straight from the jar in which it has been kept. If necessary knead in a little stock syrup to soften it up first.

If you want the fondant to be of a pouring consistency, you need to warm it with stock syrup to the correct temperature. Place a few pieces of fondant in a small bowl over a pan of hot water and add just enough stock syrup to moisten the bowl. Heat gently, stirring occasionally, and adding a few drops of food colouring if liked, until the mixture reaches 27–30 C/80–85 F on a sugar thermometer. The mixture should coat the back of a wooden spoon evenly. Use the fondant quickly to cover the cake before it begins to set; if it does set before you have managed to use it, just heat it again gently over hot water, adding a little more stock syrup.

Boiled fondant can also be used for piping. For this the consistency needs to be slightly firmer than for pouring, so you should heat it as above until just dissolved and smooth but still able to hold its shape: a spoon dipped into the fondant should leave a ribbon trail in the mixture when lifted. The fondant will not need to reach the same temperature as for pouring but if you do accidentally overheat it and it has become too thin, allow it to cool, beating continuously, until it has returned to the correct consistency. With practice you will soon be able to judge when exactly the right moment has been reached.

Kneaded fondant

This is a simpler method of making a type of fondant icing. It is generally used for modelling as it forms a smooth, pliable paste which dries firmly and holds its shape well. It can also be rolled out into a sheet and used to cover cakes.

Makes 450 g/1 lb

450 g/1 lb icing sugar
1 egg white
2 tablespoons liquid glucose, warmed

Sift the icing sugar into a bowl and make a well in the centre. Add the egg white and glucose and begin to mix the sugar into the centre with a wooden spoon. Mix until all the sugar is incorporated and the mixture is quite stiff. Knead the icing firmly on a cold worktop dusted with icing sugar until the fondant is smooth and manageable.

To colour, knead in a few drops of food colouring. If you wish to store the fondant before use, pack it into an airtight container and store in a cool place, where it will keep for 2–3 months.

Even simpler than making kneaded fondant, you can buy it ready-made. Whether bought or home-made though, kneaded fondant is not so versatile as boiled fondant – don't try to warm it with stock syrup to a pouring consistency as the egg white will coagulate. If you want to make it more pliable you can knead in a little stock syrup.

Basic Techniques

When you have assembled all the correct tools and some reliable basic recipes for cakes and icings, your next vital step is to learn the basic techniques of cake decoration.

Don't be impatient; successful icing takes skill, and skills cannot easily be achieved without time and constant practice. Before you start to apply any icing directly on to the cake, it's best to practise several times on a dummy surface first.

To practise flat icing on a smooth surface, we suggest you use a polystyrene dummy (see page 18) or a cake tin, secured upside down on a board with plasticine. If you just want to practise piping, cover a chopping board or cake board with non-stick paper or cling-film, secured underneath with tape or glue. This way, you can practise the basic piping techniques over and over, wiping away when necessary or renewing the paper. The simplest-looking techniques may often need the most practice to make perfect; straight lines, for instance. Repeat these over and over again until they are even – it may take some time.

This chapter deals in detail with all the techniques you will need when starting out on cake icing. Begin with the most basic techniques and the simplest designs, following the instructions carefully for the best results. When you've mastered these, you'll find you feel confident enough to improvise and use these techniques as a basis for your own individual designs.

As you work further through the book and try out our recipes for all types of iced cakes, you will see that all of them are based on the techniques we show you here. So, if you find you're in difficulties half way through a recipe, simply turn back and check on the techniques.

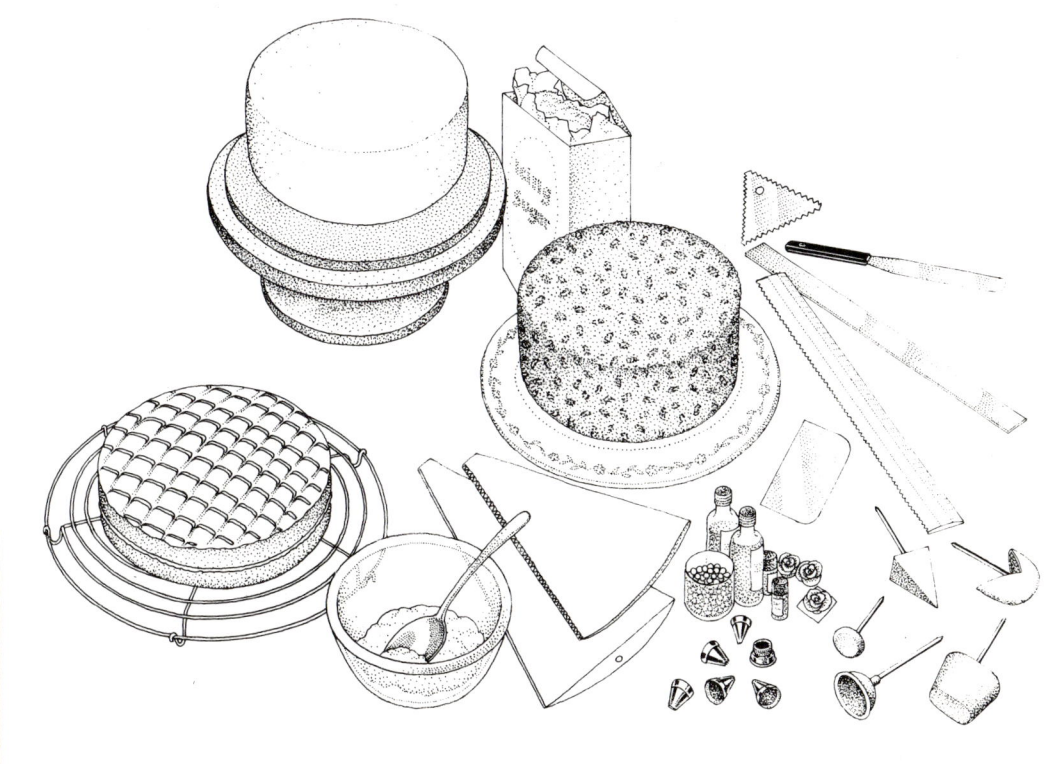

BASIC TECHNIQUES

Using an icing bag

FABRIC OR PLASTIC

Hold the bag in one hand with the nozzle pointing downwards. Turn the top over your fist to make filling easier.

Take a spoonful of icing and drop it into the bag. Do not overfill the bag – half full is enough. Any icing above that level is likely to come out of the top as you pipe. Then simply twist the top of the bag round to close it, gently pushing the icing down to the nozzle as you do so.

To pipe, grasp the icing bag with one hand where it is twisted at the top, pressing downwards with the fingers to push out the icing. Steady the bag with your other hand.

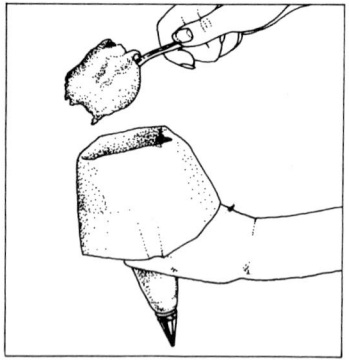

1. Put in the icing.

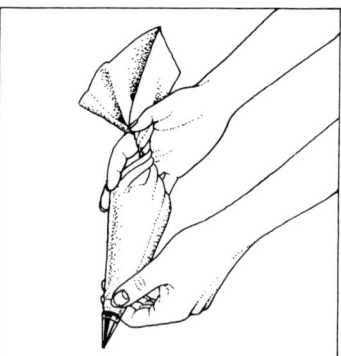

2. Twist the top to close.

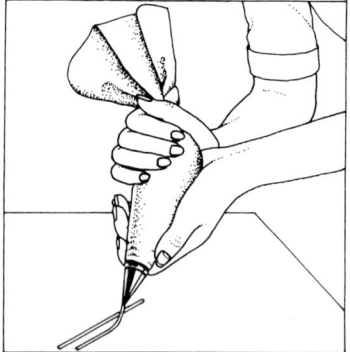

3. Test the piping for smoothness.

GREASEPROOF

Fill the bag as directed above, except that you will find the greaseproof paper too stiff to turn over your fist. To close the bag fold the two corners at the upper end to the middle, then roll the top over, easing the icing gently towards the nozzle.

We suggest two ways of piping with a greaseproof bag. Try both to find which one suits you best.

Either Hold the bag across the open fingers of one hand and press down with the thumb on the folded top to force out the icing. The other hand can be placed under the first for support.

Or Hold the bag between the fingers of both hands, forcing the icing down with the thumbs and steadying the bag with both hands at the same time.

Once the bag is filled, pipe a few lines of icing on greaseproof paper before beginning on the cake, to eliminate any air pockets and to be sure of smooth, even piping.

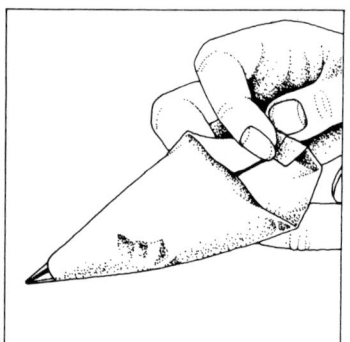

1. Fold over the top to close.

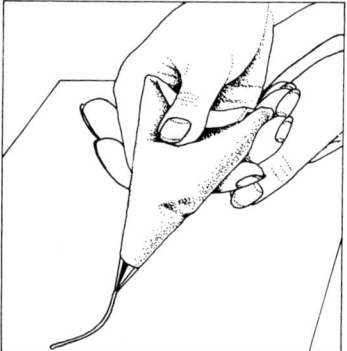
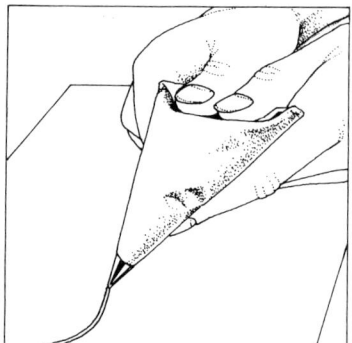

2a. and 2b. Alternative ways of holding a greaseproof bag.

BASIC TECHNIQUES

Flooding with glacé icing

Glacé icing is mainly used for 'flooding', that is coating a surface such as the top of a cake with a smooth layer of icing. For this, it is vital that the icing is of the correct spreadable consistency; it should be fairly stiff, but still just able to flow.

Pour all the icing on to the cake and, with the aid of a palette knife, spread it evenly from the centre to the edge using long, sweeping movements. If the icing runs over the edge, leave it to dry before removing it carefully with a sharp knife.

You can also use glacé icing to flood a shape outlined on the surface of a cake – a flower or a number for instance. The outline itself can be piped in glacé icing, or a different medium such as royal icing, melted chocolate, even butter cream or crème au beurre can be used to give a variety in colour and texture.

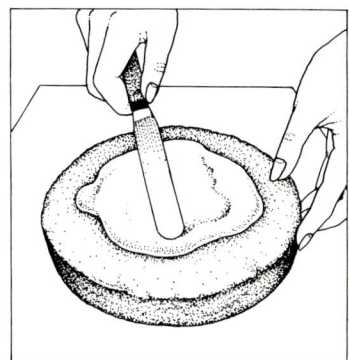

Spread the icing evenly to the edge.

Feather icing

The icing normally used for feather work is glacé icing, but you can do it with other toppings such as melted chocolate or apricot glaze and whipped cream.

Place a small quantity of the glacé icing to be used in a bowl and colour as desired with food colouring. Spoon the icing into a greaseproof piping bag without a nozzle. Pour the remaining white icing over the top of the cake, spreading quickly almost to the edge, so that it floods the cake without running over. Snip off the very tip of the greaseproof bag to allow the coloured icing to run out and, working very quickly before the icing begins to set, pipe straight parallel lines across the cake, about 1 cm ($\frac{1}{2}$ in) apart. Or you can draw a spiral from the centre of the cake out towards the edge.

Dip the tip of a sharp knife or a skewer into a jug of water and, working as quickly as you can, use it to draw straight lines, about 2.5 cm (1 in) apart, across the cake at right angles to the lines of icing. Now turn the cake round, if it helps, and intersperse these lines with lines drawn in the opposite direction, as shown, moistening the knife or skewer each time. Leave the icing to set.

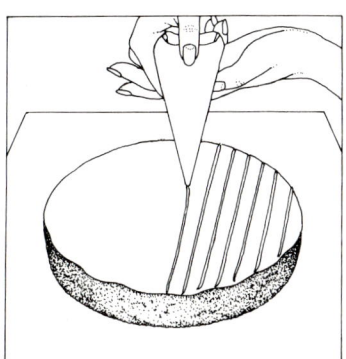

1. Pipe parallel lines across the cake.

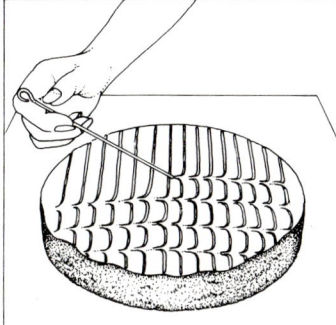

2. Draw the skewer one way.

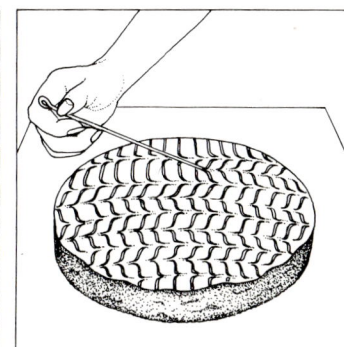

3. Draw it in the opposite direction.

Using butter cream

To sandwich a cake with butter cream, place half the butter cream on each half of the cake. Spread evenly with a palette knife almost to the edges and sandwich the two halves together. This way, the cake is held together more firmly than if the butter cream were just spread on one half.

To cover the side of a sandwich cake, spread the butter cream in a thin even layer with a palette knife. You can now leave the side as it is or coat it with nuts; sprinkle finely chopped nuts on to a sheet of greaseproof paper and, holding the cake firmly between both hands, roll it along over the nuts until evenly coated all round. Desiccated coconut and chocolate vermicelli can also be used for this. Do remember, though, that if you are intending to ice the whole cake with butter cream, you should always begin with the side.

To pipe butter cream, best results are obtained with the larger sizes of icing nozzles, or even a vegetable nozzle for a more lavish effect. Piped butter cream is ideal for special gâteaux.

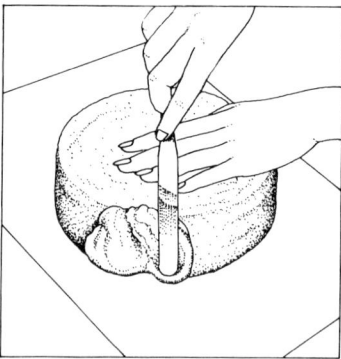

1. Spread with butter cream.

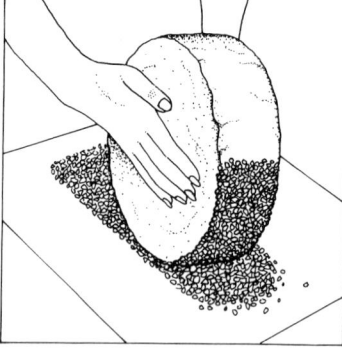

2. Roll in nuts to coat.

Applying almond paste

Almond paste is generally used as a base for royal icing, to give a smooth surface and prevent colours and oils from the cake staining the icing.

The royal icing itself needs to be spread on a level surface, so before you apply the almond paste, trim the top of the cake with a sharp knife if it has risen unevenly. Alternatively, turn the cake over and use the flat base for the top.

ROUND CAKE

Measure the circumference and the depth of the cake with pieces of string. Lightly sprinkle a work surface with sifted icing sugar.

Use two thirds of the almond paste for the side of the cake. Roll this out to a rectangle twice the depth of the cake and half the circumference and about 9 mm ($\frac{3}{8}$ in) thick. Trim the sides of the rectangle evenly using a ruler and a sharp knife. Cut the rectangle in half lengthways, to leave two equal strips.

Brush the two almond paste strips with apricot glaze. Place the cake on its side on the end of one strip, making sure that the surface you are going to use for the top of the cake is square with the edge of the paste. Roll the cake along the paste to cover half the side, joining the second strip to cover the rest. Trim away any surplus paste from the bottom edge of the cake, or press it into the base. If necessary, smooth the side by rolling a straight-sided jar against it.

On a surface lightly dusted with icing sugar, roll out the remaining third of almond paste to a round large enough for the top of the cake and about 9 mm ($\frac{3}{8}$ in) thick. Brush with apricot glaze and place the cake upside down on it. Press firmly, trimming away any surplus edges with a sharp knife.

Turn the cake the right way up and leave it for at least 24 hours before applying any icing so that the almond paste is allowed to dry out. Otherwise the oils in the paste might seep through and discolour the icing.

BASIC TECHNIQUES

1. Measure the side with string. Cut two strips of paste to fit.

2. Make sure the top of the cake is square with the paste.

3. Press the cake on to the paste round and trim away the edges.

SQUARE CAKE

Measure the length and depth of the cake sides with pieces of string or with a ruler. Sprinkle the work surface with sifted icing sugar.

Use two thirds of the almond paste for the sides of the cake; divide this into two equal portions and roll out one portion to a 9-mm (3/8-in) thick rectangle twice the depth of the cake and the length of one side. Trim the edges with the help of a ruler and a sharp knife.

Cut the rectangle in half lengthways.

Roll out, trim and cut the other portion in the same way, so that you have four equal strips of almond paste. Brush the strips evenly with apricot glaze and press the sides of the cake down on to each strip in turn, making sure again that the paste is square with what is to be the top edge of the cake. Trim away any surplus paste from the bottom edge of the cake with a sharp knife or press it into the base.

On a surface lightly dusted with icing sugar, roll out the remaining piece of almond paste to a square to fit the top of the cake, about 9 mm (3/8 in) thick. Brush it with apricot glaze and place the cake upside down on it, pressing to seal the edges of the paste firmly. Trim away any surplus paste with a sharp knife.

Turn the cake the right way up and allow the almond paste to dry out for 24 hours before icing.

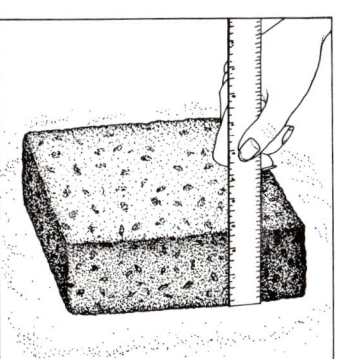
1. Measure with a ruler or string.

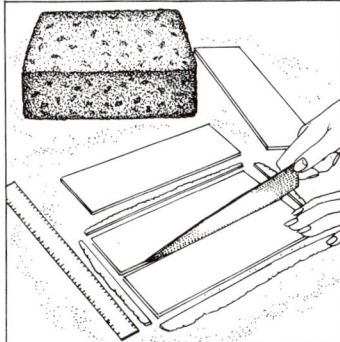
2. Cut four strips for the sides.

3. Press a side on each strip in turn.

Applying royal icing

FLAT ICING

Building up a thick, smooth coating of royal icing on a cake takes a good deal of time and a certain amount of patience. If you are icing a cake for a specific formal occasion, leave yourself plenty of time to do so, as the icing has to be applied in 2–3 thin, separate layers, allowing at least 24 hours – longer if possible – to dry out between each layer. Two layers is the absolute minimum; you will probably find you need three and more can be added if you have time. The more layers you add, the more likely you are to achieve a perfectly smooth, flat surface. It's also a good idea to ice the top and sides on separate occasions, leaving one to dry before icing the other.

Place a small spoonful of icing in the centre of the cake board and use it to fix the cake to the board. Remember that for flat icing, the consistency of the icing should be fairly soft – it should pull up into a point, but the point should just fall over. If necessary, thin it with a little egg white or beat in some sifted icing sugar to stiffen it.

Place the cake on a turntable if you have one: improvise one if you haven't (see page 14). Put about one third of the icing allowed for your first layer on top of the cake and, using a palette knife, spread it evenly over the surface of the cake with a paddling motion to eliminate air bubbles. Place your other hand on the turntable to steady it if necessary.

Hold an icing ruler or a long palette knife at an angle of 45° to the cake and, without pressing too hard, draw it straight across the icing towards you to smooth the surface. Don't worry if this first layer is not completely flat. It isn't easy to achieve an absolutely smooth surface with almond paste and at this initial stage, some unevenness may well show through the icing.

Trim any surplus icing from the edge of the cake with a clean palette knife and leave the top to dry for 24 hours.

When the icing is dry, examine it for any roughness in the surface and gently remove it, if necessary, with a piece of fine emery paper or a sharp knife. Now begin on the sides.

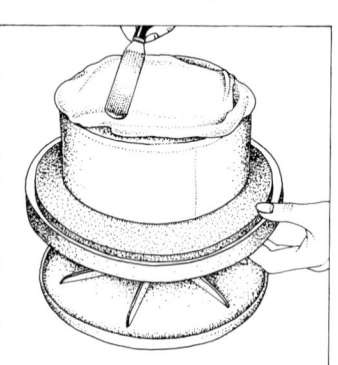
1. Spread one third of the royal icing on top of the cake.

2. Draw an icing ruler across at an angle of 45° to smooth.

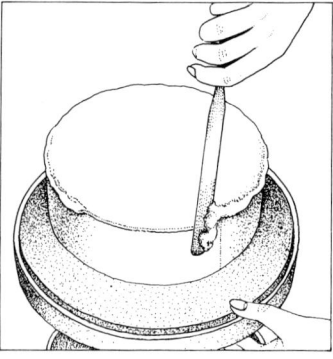
3. Trim the edges with a palette knife.

4. Smooth the icing on the side of the cake with an icing comb.

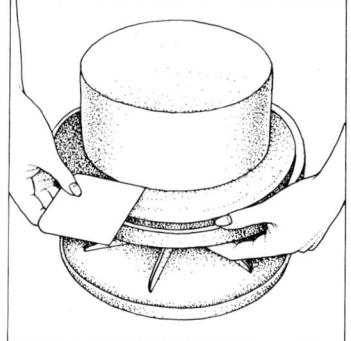
5. Use the comb at a different angle to smooth the icing on the board.

BASIC TECHNIQUES

For a round cake, spread the remaining two thirds of the icing all around the side, using a palette knife in a paddling action as before. Hold a smooth-edged icing comb or ruler with one hand against the side at an angle of 45° and, turning the turntable with the other hand, pull the comb or ruler over the side to smooth the icing. Trim away any icing that is forced over the top edge of the cake.

For a square cake, apply the icing to one side at a time, smoothing with a comb or ruler and turning the cake each time. Or, to be even surer of a good result, you can apply the icing to opposite sides in pairs, allowing one pair to dry completely for 24 hours before icing the other. This is because if all the sides are wet at the same time, you may find it difficult to smooth one with an icing comb or ruler without touching the adjoining ones.

After all the sides of the cake have dried for at least 24 hours, smooth down any roughness in the icing with emery paper or a sharp knife as before. Then begin the whole process all over again.

It can look better on formal cakes if the icing is taken over the cake board itself. When you have finished your final layer of icing, leave the cake to dry for 24 hours, then spread an even layer of icing over the board with a palette knife. Using a smooth comb or a palette knife held at an angle to the board, smooth off the icing as before, turning the turntable as you go.

Once you have applied all the layers to each side of the cake, leave the icing to dry for at least 48 hours before applying any further decoration.

ROUGH ICING

Rough icing is associated chiefly with royal icing, but butter cream, fudge icing and American frosting also lend themselves well to it. When used with royal icing it can create a magical, snow-like effect, which makes it a popular way of decorating less formal Christmas cakes. It has the advantage too of needing much less time and care than flat icing; you can apply it to the cake as late as Christmas Eve if necessary and it should still be ready for the day itself.

Mix the icing until it is stiff enough to hold firm peaks. Spoon it all on top of the cake, completely covering the top and sides. Using the tip of a palette knife, pull up peaks of icing to form rough points. Set any decorations (moulded almond paste or fondant figures, for instance) in the icing while it is still wet: it should be stiff enough to hold them.

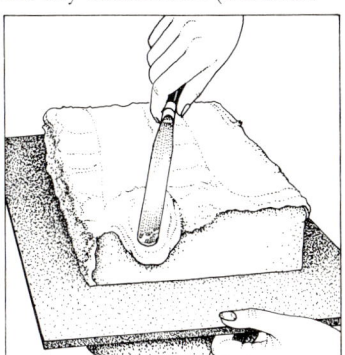

1. Cover the cake in icing.

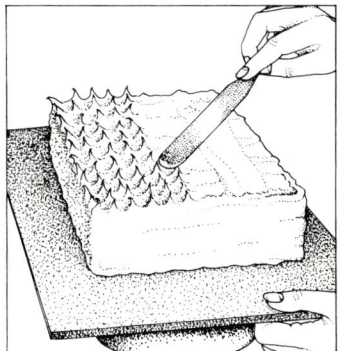

2. Pull the icing up into peaks.

BASIC TECHNIQUES

Making a template

Before starting to pipe a design on top of a cake it's advisable to plan it carefully and work it out on paper first. You can then make a greaseproof paper pattern or 'template' to transfer your design on to the cake.

First work out your design roughly on a piece of paper. A cake marker (see page 17) will help you draw curved designs symmetrically.

Cut a piece of greaseproof paper to the exact size of the top of the cake, whether it's round or square. To make sure each section of the cake is marked equally, fold the paper into quarters or eighths, folding each time from the centre point.

Copy a section of your planned design on to the edge of the folded paper and cut along the outline. Your outline can be star-shaped, as here, or composed of curves, deep or shallow, or any other kind of shape you like. (If you are planning a more complicated design with several different patterns, copy a section of it on to the paper as directed, and mark it through all the layers of paper with a series of pin pricks.)

Open the paper out and you should see your basic design. You now have a template which you can use as it is, or, to make it easier to work with as well as longer-lasting, you could transfer it to a piece of card. Place the paper shape on top of the card and carefully draw round it. Cut the card with sharp scissors, and your template is ready to use.

Position the template on the cake (make sure the icing has dried out completely first) and hold it firmly in place. Mark the outline of the template on to the icing by pricking round the shape with a pin or lightly scratching the surface. Remove the template and your design should be clearly marked on top of the cake. When icing, be sure to cover the marks.

Using this method you should be able, with practice, to build up quite complicated designs without any difficulty. You can transfer patterns, lettering or numbering on to both top and sides of a cake, using the appropriate templates, so that they can be piped directly onto the icing. Some basic designs, letters and patterns which you can trace directly can be found on pages 53–56 and on the endpapers.

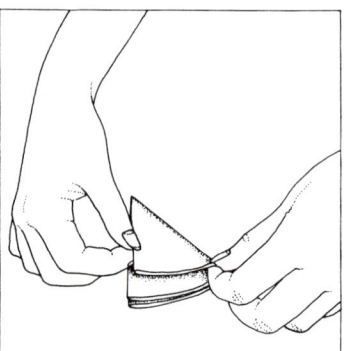

1. Fold the paper into even sections.

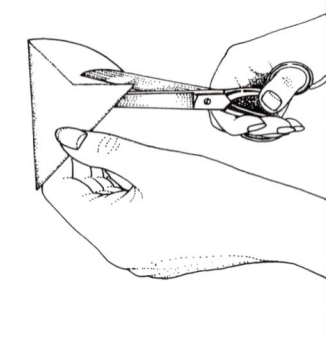

2. Cut along the outline of your design.

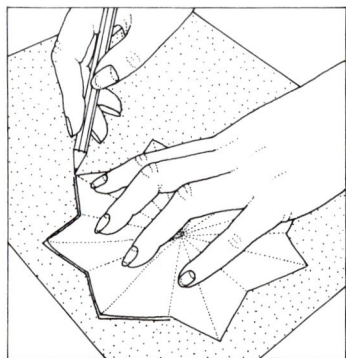

3. Transfer the template to card for extra strength.

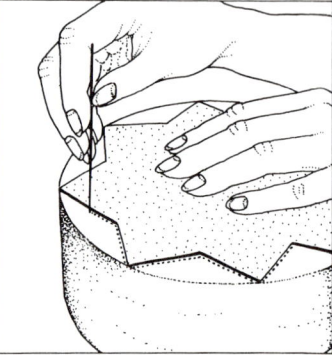

4. A hat pin is ideal for marking the shape on the cake.

Piping techniques

Using a star nozzle

Star nozzles vary greatly in size and in the number of points they have. This of course affects the appearance of the piping. A 5-point or 8-point nozzle is the most useful size to begin with. You can use a star nozzle for royal icing, butter cream and crème au beurre as these icings are all soft enough to pipe, but strong enough to hold the star shape.

To pipe stars, hold the tube vertically above the cake, the nozzle almost touching the surface. Press out a little icing. Once a star is formed, release the pressure and lift the nozzle quickly. If you don't lift it quickly enough, you may leave a 'tail' of icing in the centre of the star.

A star nozzle will also make rosettes. Begin as if you were piping a star but as you squeeze, move the nozzle in a small spiral, finishing in the middle of the rosette. Again, pull away quickly to avoid leaving a 'tail'.

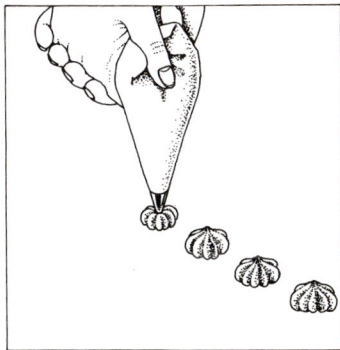
Press out icing for a star.

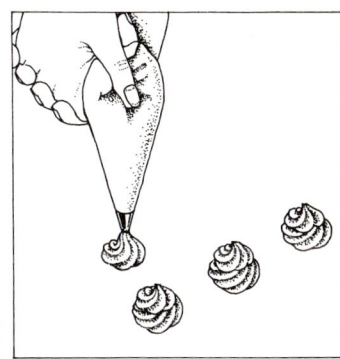
Rotate the nozzle slightly for a rosette.

Shell piping

Like stars, shells can be piped in royal icing, butter cream and crème au beurre.

To pipe a shell, hold the icing bag at an angle to the surface of the cake with the flat part of the shell nozzle on the underside. Press the icing out gently while pushing the bag slightly away from you, then pull towards you and release the pressure at the same time so that a 'tail' is formed on the cake.

To make a border of shell, pipe the next shell just over the tail of the last, continuing evenly until the border is complete.

If you don't have a shell nozzle, you can pipe shells with a star nozzle, using the same action as above. The result will not make such a good shell shape but still be quite satisfactory.

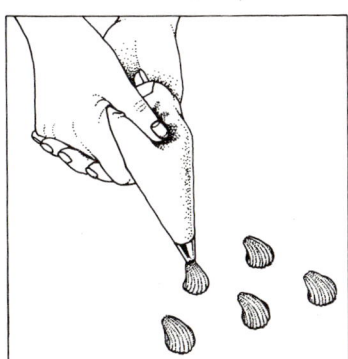
Pull towards you to form a shell.

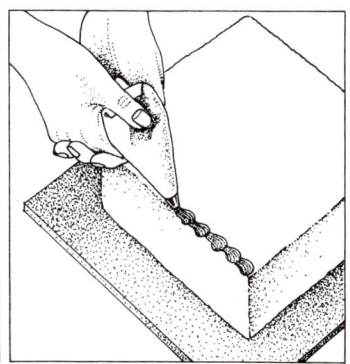
Piping a shell border.

BASIC TECHNIQUES

Trellis piping

Trellis can be piped straight on to a cake for a decorative effect, or on to a mould to build up a raised design which, once dried, can be transferred to the cake. Depending on what mould you use you can make a pyramid, basket or cradle of delicate trellis work. Only royal icing is suitable for this as no other icing will dry hard enough to retain the shape of the mould.

PIPING ON TO A CAKE

Mark out the area to be covered on the cake with a template and a pin. Using a plain writing nozzle, pipe a single fine line of royal icing round the outline of the shape.

Pipe a straight line across the centre of the shape from one edge to the opposite. Pipe lines across parallel to the first, about 5 mm ($\frac{1}{4}$ in) apart.

Now turn the cake so that you can pipe another series of parallel lines over the top of the first. Pipe either at right angles to the first layer to form squares, or on the diagonal to form diamond shapes.

Allow the trellis to dry thoroughly for 24 hours.

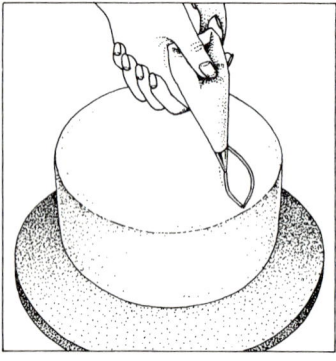
1. Outline the shape in royal icing.

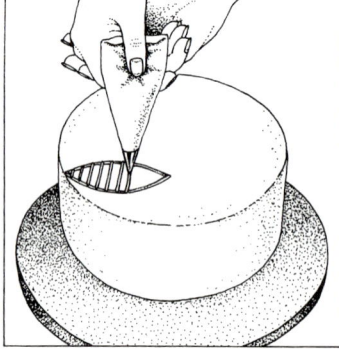
2. Pipe lines across the shape.

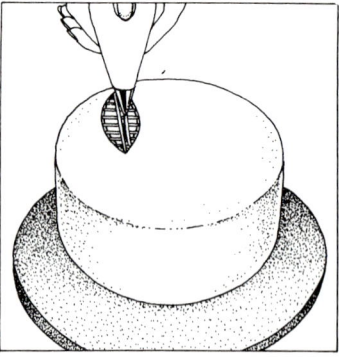
3. Pipe in the opposite direction.

USING A MOULD

Grease the mould lightly by brushing it with melted lard or oil. Pipe a single line all round the base to support the trellis work. Turning the mould gradually around between the fingers and thumb of one hand, pipe lines from the base line to the very top of the mould so that all lines meet at the centre.

Now either pipe lines parallel to the base line encircling the mould from bottom to top, or pipe them diagonally over the mould to form diamond shapes.

Leave to dry for at least 24 hours, then carefully remove the shape from the mould.

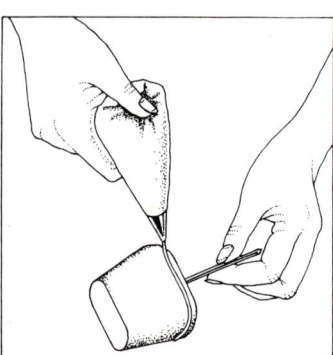
1. Pipe a line of icing round the base.

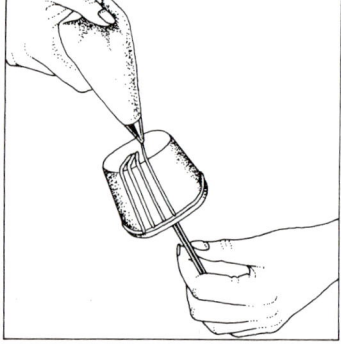
2. Pipe lines to meet at the top of the mould.

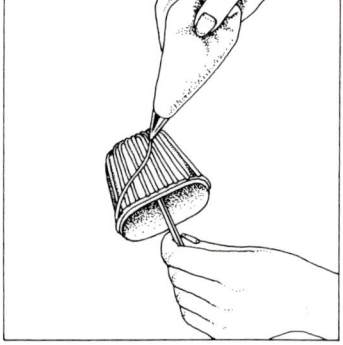
3. Pipe over the mould in a different direction.

Piping flowers

Flowers made from royal icing are classic decorations on formal cakes. You can make them well in advance and keep them in a tin for several months.

PIPING A ROSE

Dab a little royal icing on top of an icing nail and fix a small square of non-stick or greaseproof paper on top.

Put a small quantity of royal icing into a bag fitted with a petal nozzle. Holding the nail upright with one hand, position the bag at right angles to the surface of the nail, the nozzle touching the centre of the paper, with the thin part of the nozzle uppermost. Gently squeeze out a little icing, turning the nail at the same time so that a cone of icing is formed in the centre of the paper. Press the nozzle down sideways to finish off the cone, release pressure and pull away quickly.

Now position the nozzle, thin part still uppermost, at a slight angle leaning outwards from the cone and pipe a petal in a fan movement around the cone, turning the nail gently as you pipe. Press the nozzle down sideways as before, release pressure and lift off quickly. Continue in this way, making five or six overlapping petals. The size of the rose can be varied by varying the number of petals.

Lift the paper holding the finished rose from the nail and leave it to dry completely in a warm, damp-free place for at least 24 hours before removing it from the paper. In this way you can make a large number of roses at a time, using only one icing nail.

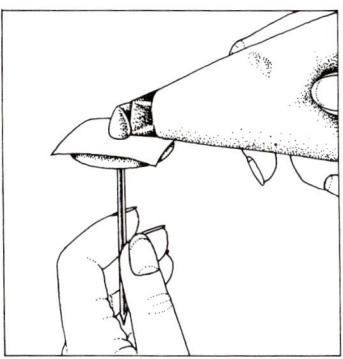

1. Pipe a cone of royal icing on the icing nail.

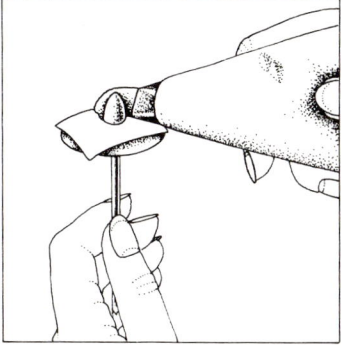

2. Pipe a petal in a fan shape around the cone.

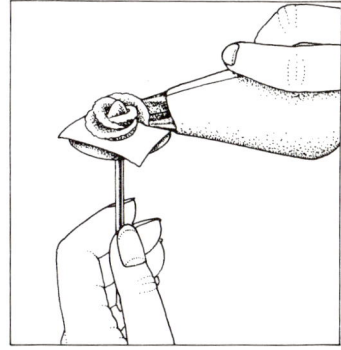

3. Finish each petal by pressing the nozzle down sideways.

PIPING A DAISY

Fix a square of greaseproof or non-stick paper to the top of an icing nail with a dab of icing. Using an icing bag fitted with a petal nozzle, hold the bag vertically above the nail, the nozzle touching the paper, with the widest side of the nozzle towards the centre.

Pipe out a very small amount of icing, release pressure and lift off quickly. Turn the nail and pipe another blob next to the first. Pipe five or more even-sized petals, pointing equally out from the centre, just touching each other.

Complete the centre of the daisy by placing a silver ball in it, or by piping a small dot of yellow royal icing with a plain writing nozzle.

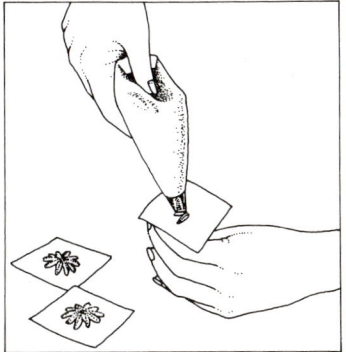

1. Pipe blobs of icing pointing out from the centre of the nail.

Making run-outs

A run-out is a shape such as a flower, animal, letter, number or any other motif, which is initially outlined in icing before being flooded to the edges with more icing of the same or a different colour. You can either pipe a run-out directly on to the cake or – if you are a beginner or the design is complicated – it may be safer to make it first on waxed or non-stick paper, transferring it to the cake when dry.

The icing to use for a run-out which is being piped directly on to a cake can be either glacé or royal icing; if you are making the run-out separately however, you should use royal icing only, as glacé icing will not set hard enough for the run-out to be transferred from one place to another.

To make a run-out on waxed or non-stick paper, draw your chosen design on a piece of card. Place a sheet of non-stick or waxed paper over the drawing and secure it in place with dabs of icing to prevent it moving as you work. Using a No. 1 or 2 plain writing nozzle pipe a continuous line of royal icing round the outline of the shape as it appears through the paper, enclosing it completely with a neat join.

Slightly thin down some of the royal icing with water or egg white until it will just coat the back of a spoon. Using a teaspoon, drop a little of the thinner icing into the centre of the shape. With the aid of a skewer or a fine paint brush, quickly ease the icing around the inside of the shape until all the corners are filled. Prick out any air bubbles with a skewer. The shape should be quite full but not enough to overflow.

Slide the piece of waxed or non-stick paper off the card and leave the run-out to dry in a warm, dry place for at least 24 hours before attempting to remove it from the paper itself. Large run-outs may need 2–3 days to dry out. It is always advisable to make extra ones in case of breakages.

When the run-out is completely dry, you can remove it from the paper. The safest way to do this is to place the sheet of paper holding the run-out on a thick board or a book; then, steadying the paper on one side of the run-out with one hand, carefully pull the paper towards the edge of the book with the other, easing the run-out gently from the paper as it reaches the edge.

Place the run-out in position on the cake and secure it with a dab of royal icing.

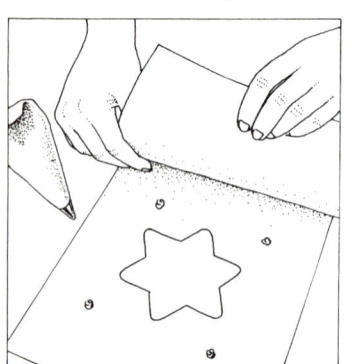
1. Fix waxed paper over the design.

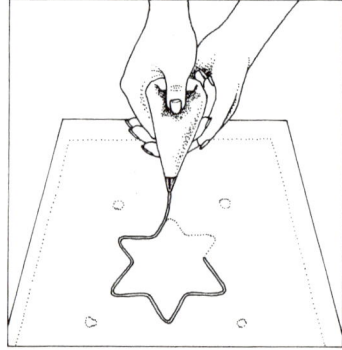
2. Outline the shape in royal icing.

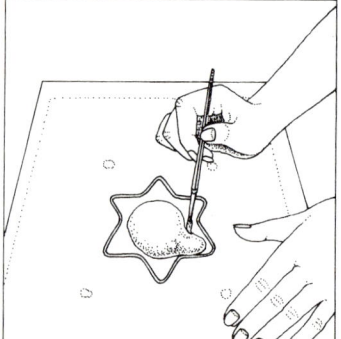
3. Ease icing around the inside.

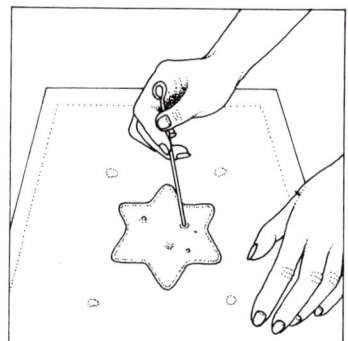
4. Prick air bubbles with a skewer.

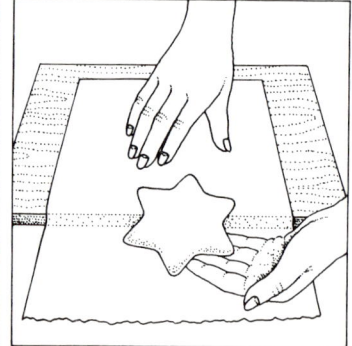
5. Gently remove the dried run-out.

Lettering and numbering

The run-out technique is often used to give depth to writing or numbering on cakes, whether piped directly on to the cake or set first on non-stick paper as before.

In order to pipe a number straight on to the cake, make a template first by drawing your chosen design on a piece of greaseproof paper. You can trace one from the samples given on page 56 if you like.

Place the template on the cake and mark round the outline with a pin. Remove the template and pipe round the outline with royal icing, taking care to cover all the pin pricks. Thin down some icing to a flooding consistency and fill in the shape evenly, pricking out any air bubbles with a skewer. Leave the run-out to dry.

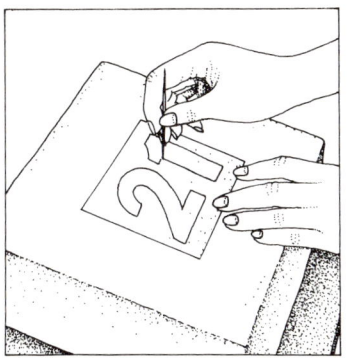

1. Mark your design with a pin.

2. Pipe along the pin marks.

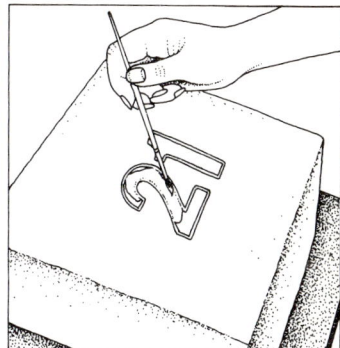

3. Fill in the numbers evenly.

Making almond paste decorations

Almond paste is a very versatile material to use for cake decoration. It can be rolled, coloured, cut and moulded and will hold its shape indefinitely if treated correctly.

The main consideration when working with almond paste is that it becomes progressively more oily with handling; take care not to overknead it or you will find it difficult to work with. If it does become sticky, dust the work surface and your hands with sifted icing sugar. But if left uncovered, almond paste quickly dries out making it brittle and impossible to shape. If this happens, try moistening it with a few drops of glucose or glycerine.

You can colour almond paste with edible food colourings by kneading in a few drops at a time until evenly distributed. To prevent your hands being coloured, too, try kneading the paste inside a polythene bag. Alternatively, the food colouring can be painted on to the almond paste after shaping, diluted with a little water if a paler shade is wanted.

CUTTING SHAPES

Sprinkle some icing sugar over a work surface and, using a rolling pin, roll out the almond paste to the required thickness. Cut the paste into the shapes you want using fancy cutters, or a template and a sharp knife. You may find it helpful to dust the edges of the cutter or knife with icing sugar first if the paste is sticky.

Holly leaves can be made by using the wide base of a nozzle to outline the curved shapes of the leaves. You can then mark the impression of the veins on the leaves with a sharp knife.

Leave the shapes on a flat surface or on non-stick paper to dry and harden before placing them on the cake. If almond paste decorations are placed on royal icing before they are dry, the colour can run and spoil the icing.

BASIC TECHNIQUES

MODELLING

Simple figures, fruits, animals and flowers can be made by colouring and shaping almond paste.

Orange, lemon, lime Colour the paste with the appropriate food colourings before shaping it into small balls. For lemons and limes slightly elongate the shapes, nipping together each end with your finger tips. For an orange, stick a clove into the top. Roll the fruits over a fine grater to mark the surface.

Apple, pear Colour the paste a pale green and roll into a ball or pear shape. Break a clove in half and stick the round end into the base of the fruit and the pointed end into the top to form a stem. A little pink or red colouring can be painted on the sides for a rosy blush.

Grapes Colour the paste green and shape a small piece into a triangle. Roll the rest into tiny balls and stick them on to the triangle. Use a clove for a stalk.

Strawberry Colour the paste red, shape it into a ball and roll it to elongate slightly at one end. Then roll the strawberry over a fine grater to mark the surface. Colour some more paste green, shape it into a leafy hull and stick it on top.

Father Christmas Mould a round body from red almond paste. Roll out two short pieces of red paste for arms and stick them on the body. Colour a little almond paste pink and shape it into a round head and tiny round hands. Place these on the body. Cut a thin triangle of red paste and join two points round together to form a hat with the third point at the top. Place it on the head. Using a piping bag fitted with a plain nozzle, pipe a face, beard and trimmings in white royal icing on the Father Christmas.

Flowers Colour the paste as required. To make a simple flower, divide the paste up according to the number of petals you want and roll the pieces into balls. Press and mould each between finger and thumb to form a petal shape and join the petals in an overlapping circle. Using yellow almond paste, form a tiny round centre or separate stamens to finish the flower.

To make a rose, begin by moulding a small piece of coloured almond paste into a cone for the centre. Shape petals as before and wrap them around the cone, overlapping and curving slightly outwards. Pinch the rose at the base so all the petals hold together.

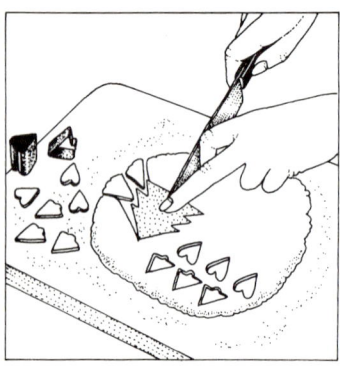
Cut-outs

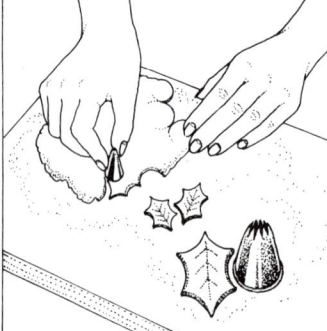
Holly leaves

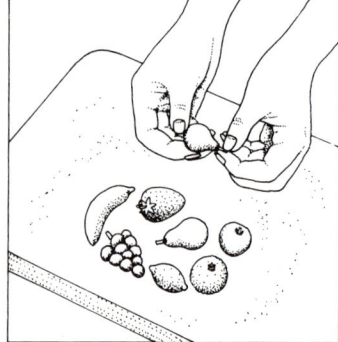
Fruits

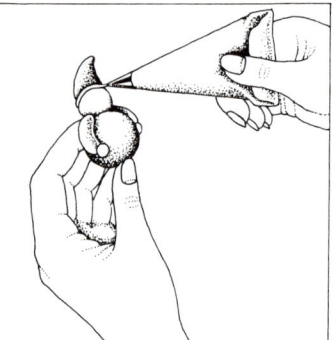
Father Christmas

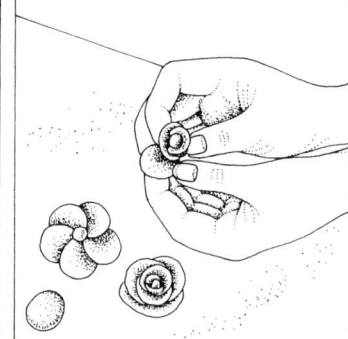
Simple flower and rose

BASIC TECHNIQUES

Modelling with fondant icing

Fondant icing makes an extremely pliable medium for shaping into cake decorations. It is a soft icing which can be handled easily, but stores well and dries firm on exposure to air. It can be moulded into the same shapes as almond paste, but being white, has greater possibilities for colouring. You can use it as it is, for Christmas roses for instance, or you can colour it into much clearer, purer colours than can be achieved with almond paste.

Knead the fondant until pliable and colour as desired with food colourings. Keep any icing not being used immediately in a sealed container or cover with a damp cloth to prevent it drying out.

CHRISTMAS ROSE

Roll out the fondant on a surface lightly dusted with icing sugar. Cut out five small rounds using the base of an icing or a vegetable nozzle, depending on what size you want the rose to be. Mould each round between finger and thumb, slightly pinching one side to form thin, curved petals. Arrange the petals against the sides of a patty tin to dry, so that they harden into a gently curving shape. Allow to dry in a warm place for 48 hours.

When the petals are firm, pipe a little white royal icing on the slightly pointed side of one petal and use it to attach the next; continue to build up the flower. Pipe tiny stamens in the centre of the rose in yellow royal icing.

Daffodil 1. Cut out six petal shapes and a strip for the trumpet.

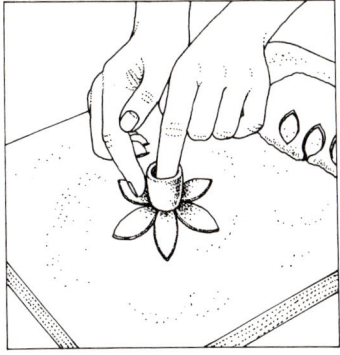

2. Arrange the petals around the trumpet and leave to dry.

DAFFODIL

Colour the fondant yellow. Roll it out thinly and cut six petal shapes with a sharp knife. Leave these on one side.

Cut a long strip of fondant for the trumpet and mould it around your finger in a tube shape, sealing the join. Press one end of the tube together to form the base of the trumpet. Moisten the base slightly and arrange the petals around it in a flower shape. Leave the daffodil to dry on a flat surface covered with non-stick paper. Alternatively, for a more curved shape, stand it in a patty tin to dry.

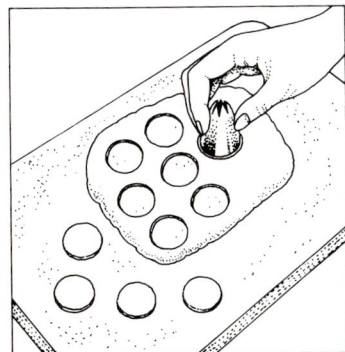

Christmas rose 1. Cut out rounds with the base of a nozzle.

2. Arrange the petals to dry on a curved surface.

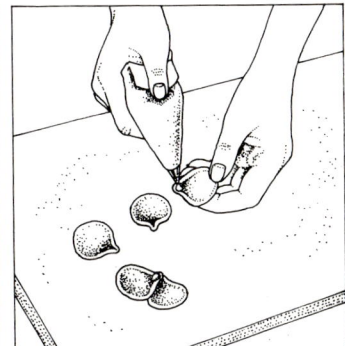

3. Stick the petals together into a rose shape with royal icing.

Simple chocolate work

Types of chocolate vary in many characteristics, so before you buy any, think carefully about what you're going to use it for.

The kind we would suggest principally for cake decoration is dark, bitter, cooking chocolate – not to be confused with chocolate-flavoured cake covering, which is often wrongly referred to as cooking chocolate. Real cooking chocolate can be obtained from specialist shops; it has a less sweet, more chocolaty flavour than the dessert variety and does not need quite so much care when being melted, as it can stand higher temperatures before being spoiled.

Even better than ordinary cooking chocolate is Couverture; this is considerably more expensive, but you can buy it in chocolate-dot form if you only need a small amount. Being high in cocoa butter, it gives a very smooth, glossy appearance and has a good, strong chocolate flavour. Couverture often has to be 'tempered', which involves heating to a specific temperature and cooling again before use; instructions on the packet will tell you how to do this.

Dessert chocolate is more widely available than either of the above, and if melted carefully, gives perfectly good results. You can use plain or milk, according to taste, but as a rule the chocolate with the fewest additives will have the strongest flavour and will melt most smoothly.

Finally, chocolate-flavoured cake covering, milk or plain, is not strictly chocolate, but it's much cheaper and quite satisfactory for all general cooking and icing purposes. You will notice the difference in flavour though if you use it to make chocolate decorations. It also dries to a duller finish than real chocolate.

When working with chocolate, your room temperature should ideally be around 65 F (18 C), so avoid very hot days or frosty winter conditions. Heat will obviously soften the chocolate, while damp conditions can dull it.

MELTING CHOCOLATE

Always take great care when melting chocolate, particularly if you are using dessert chocolate. Heat and moisture can spoil the texture very easily, making the chocolate impossible to work with.

Roughly chop the chocolate or grate it into a dry bowl. Place the bowl in a warm place (such as an airing cupboard or a low oven), or over a pan of hot, not boiling, water. The water should not touch the bowl. Heat very gently, stirring occasionally until the chocolate is melted and smooth. If the water boils, not only might the chocolate overheat, but steam might condense on it – either of which will harden the chocolate. For most decorating purposes, the chocolate should reach a temperature of about 85 F (30 C).

MAKING CARAQUE

The fine, delicate rolls of chocolate known as caraque make a classic decoration on rich chocolate cakes. Ideally, caraque should be made on a marble slab to keep it cool, but you can use a smooth, clean formica worktop instead, either as it is or covered with a sheet of non-stick paper anchored down well.

Melt the chocolate and spread it in a thick layer quickly and evenly over the work surface. Leave it until just set, then push a sharp, straight-bladed knife across the chocolate at an angle of 45°, scraping off thin curls as you go. Chill the caraque until firm.

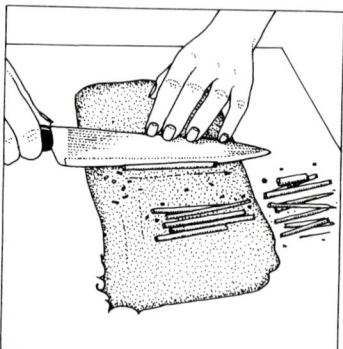

Caraque

MAKING CHOCOLATE CURLS

This is a quick method of imitating caraque.

Take a bar of chocolate (or break off a few squares if you find it easier) and scrape a vegetable peeler or paring knife across the smooth side to give small chocolate curls.

BASIC TECHNIQUES

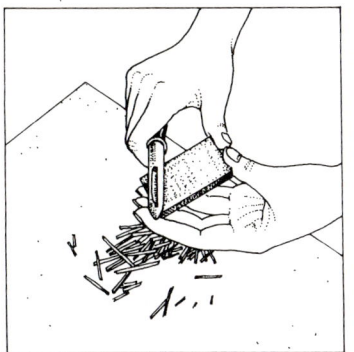
Chocolate curls or quick caraque

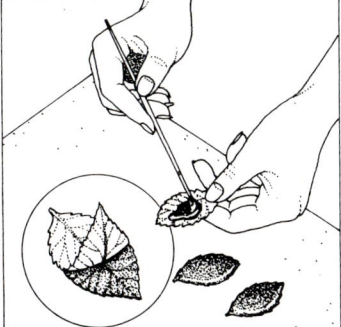
Leaves

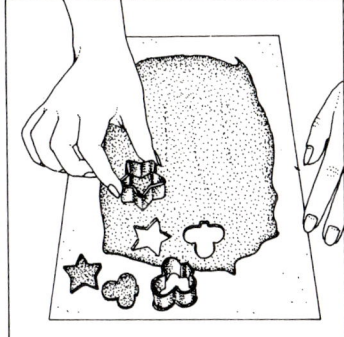
Cut-outs

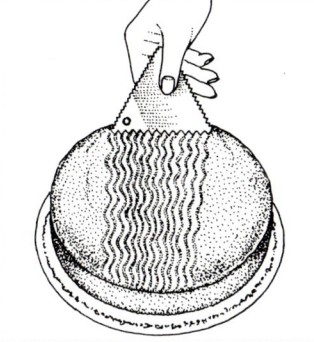
Combing technique

CUTTING CHOCOLATE SHAPES

Melt the chocolate and spread it in a thin, even layer over a sheet of waxed or non-stick paper. Leave it until just set. Cut into shapes, using fancy cutters or a sharp knife. Chill until firm.

PIPING CHOCOLATE SHAPES

This is a way of making run-outs (see page 46), but using chocolate instead of royal icing.

Draw your design on a piece of card and place a sheet of waxed or non-stick paper over the top. Fill a greaseproof icing bag with melted chocolate and snip off the very tip with scissors to allow a thin stream of chocolate to run out. The chocolate should flow out without any pressure. Follow the outline of the design through the paper and fill it in or leave it open as desired. Leave to set and peel off the paper carefully.

COMBING CHOCOLATE

For a simple 'combed' effect on a cake, pour melted chocolate in a thin layer over the top and spread it evenly with a palette knife. Just as the chocolate is beginning to set, run a serrated icing comb over it, making a wavy pattern. Leave to set.

MAKING CHOCOLATE LEAVES

Choose clean and unblemished fresh leaves as moulds for your chocolate ones. Rose leaves are the most popular as they are firm and have a simple, basic leaf shape. You could also try using holly leaves for a variation.

Melt the chocolate and paint a thin, even layer on the underside of each leaf, spreading right to the edges. Place them on a flat surface covered with waxed paper and leave to dry completely. When set, use the tip of a knife to lever the chocolate away from the leaves. You will find that the leaf veins are delicately marked on the chocolate. Store in a cool place until needed.

BASIC TECHNIQUES

Crystallising flowers

Crystallised flowers and leaves make attractive decorations on all kinds of cakes and are very simple to make. Violets, apple and cherry blossom, primroses, rose petals, mint and rose leaves, even sprigs of heather are all good for crystallising. With any other kind of flower or leaf, be sure to check first that it is edible and in particular, avoid using any flowers grown from bulbs, as many of these can be poisonous. Make sure the leaves and flowers you do use are clean, dry and fresh and have no blemishes.

METHOD 1

1 egg white
caster sugar.

Lightly beat the egg white with a fork until frothy. Holding the flower or leaf between your fingertips or with tweezers, dip it into the egg white to coat it completely, allowing any excess to run off. Sprinkle with caster sugar, shake off excess and arrange on a tray lined with greaseproof paper; allow to dry in a warm, dry place such as an airing cupboard. It may take anything from two to 24 hours to dry, depending on the atmospheric conditions and the type of flower.

Store in a screw-topped jar and use within six weeks.

METHOD 2

15 g/½ oz gum arabic
2 tablespoons rose water
caster sugar

Mix the gum arabic and rose water together in a bowl. Cover and leave to dissolve for about 2 hours.

Paint the mixture over the flower or leaf, coating all surfaces. Sprinkle with caster sugar, shaking off any excess. Place on a tray lined with non-stick paper and leave to dry in a warm place for at least 24 hours. A second sprinkling of caster sugar can be added if desired.

Flowers and leaves crystallised by this method should keep for several months if stored in an airtight container.

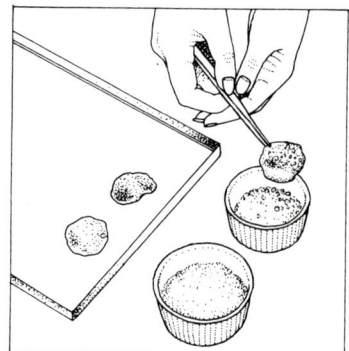
Method 1: Using egg white.

Method 2: Using gum arabic.

Extras to buy

Apart from the decorations you can make at home, there is a large selection of commercial cake decorations which you can choose from. Nearly all the ones listed below will keep in your store cupboard for several months, so it's worth building up a good supply. The only ones which are better bought in for specific occasions are the chocolate decorations, as these (except for the vermicelli) do not keep so well, and chocolate coffee beans in particular are not always easily available.

silver sugar balls
mimosa balls
edible sugar flowers
chocolate vermicelli
sugar hundreds and thousands
chocolate coffee beans
chocolate dots
chocolate buttons
crystallised violets and rose petals
angelica
glacé cherries
edible food colourings

Stockists for many of these items as well as for the more specialised trimmings such as pillars, horseshoes, bells and so on, can be found listed on page 125.

BASIC TECHNIQUES

TEMPLATE DESIGNS

Here is a selection of figures and shapes for you to trace directly to make templates for decorating your cakes. Some of these are used in various cake designs given in Iced Cakes for all Occasions (pages 57–122); others we hope will inspire you in creating your own ideas.

A complete range of letters and numbers to trace can also be found on the endpapers at either end of this book.

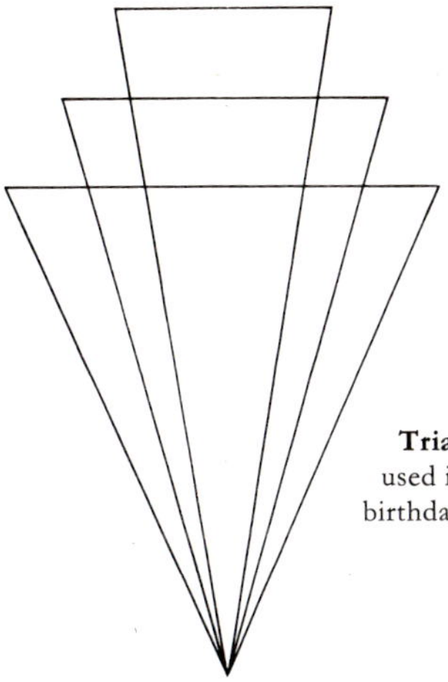

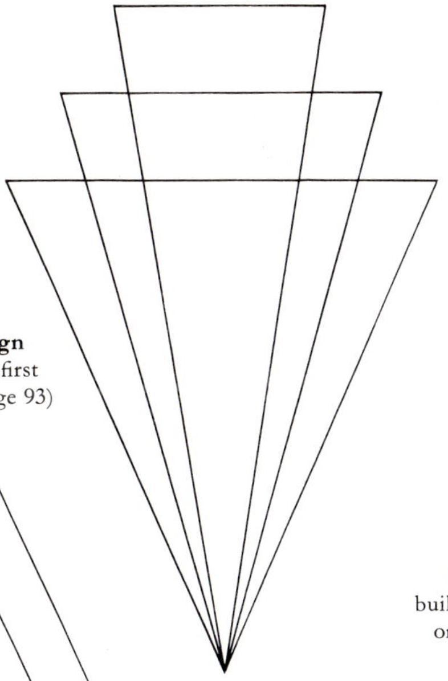

Triangle design
used in Twenty-first birthday cake (page 93)

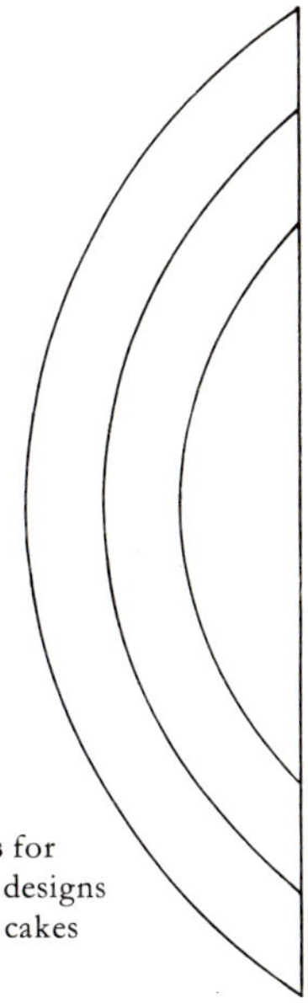

Scallops for building up designs on formal cakes

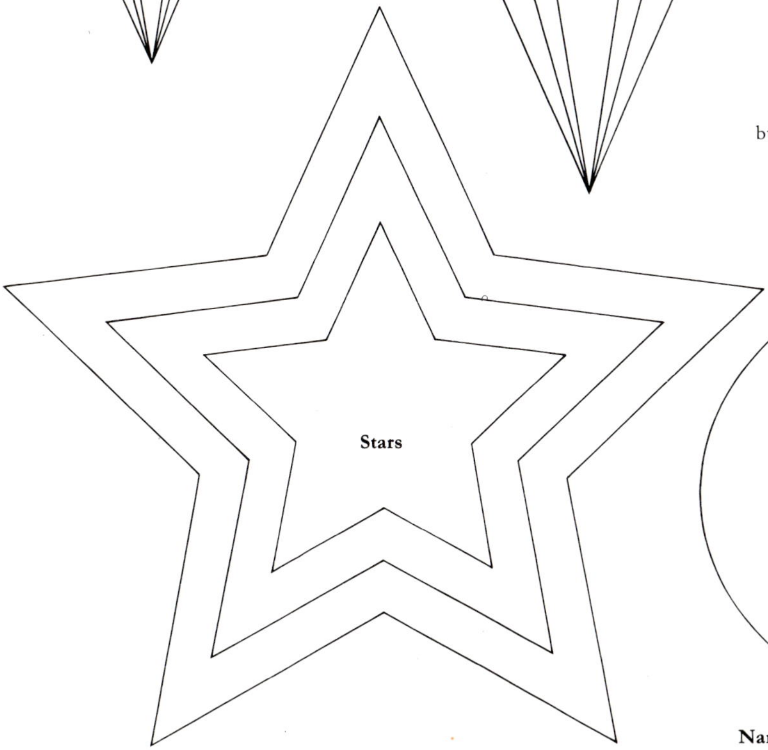

Stars

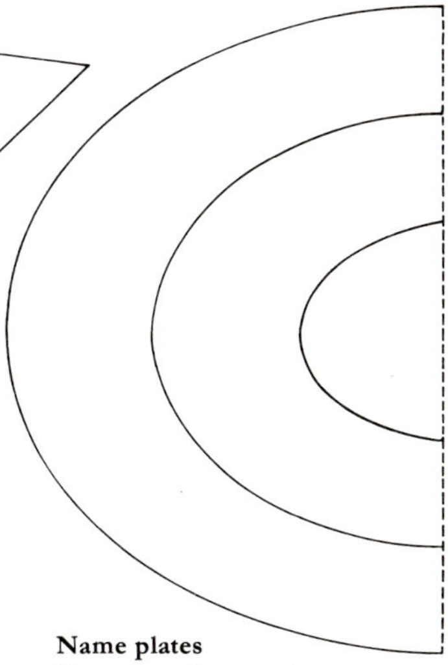

Name plates
Trace these shapes twice to form complete ovals on which to write names.

BASIC TECHNIQUES

Doves

Hearts

Gingerbread man

Rabbit

BASIC TECHNIQUES

BASIC TECHNIQUES

12345
67890

Merry Christmas

Happy Birthday

Anniversary

Best Wishes

Iced Cakes for all Occasions

Now that you've assembled all the equipment, learned the basic techniques and armed yourself with a number of reliable recipes, it's time to put it all together and start creating your first masterpiece.

This chapter combines those skills and basic recipes dealt with earlier in a selection of specially designed cakes for you to try. These are arranged according to the kind of occasion when a cake might be called for: Teatime cakes, Gâteaux, Celebration cakes for birthdays, Christmas and other times of the year, Formal cakes for weddings and christenings and last – but not least – Children's party cakes. Within these sections the whole spectrum of cake icing is covered, the techniques used ranging from the simplest flooding and rough icing to the more delicate trellis and filigree work. Depending on the time you have and the effect you want to create, you can choose whether your Christmas cake is going to show a colourful Christmas scene in run-out work, or simply be rough-iced into a snowy effect. Above all, don't be frightened by any of the designs; what looks most difficult and delicate really just needs time, practice and a steady hand – and meanwhile you can settle for one of the simpler ones. Don't forget that you don't have to stick absolutely to the ideas given here; the instructions have been made as precise as possible merely to guide you. You can always design your own cakes, making use of those techniques you're happiest with.

Whichever cake you may choose to try out, however simple or complicated, make full use of the skills you've acquired and combine them with your own creative ideas. Above all, have the confidence to try – you can always refer back to the basic information in the previous chapters if you come unstuck!

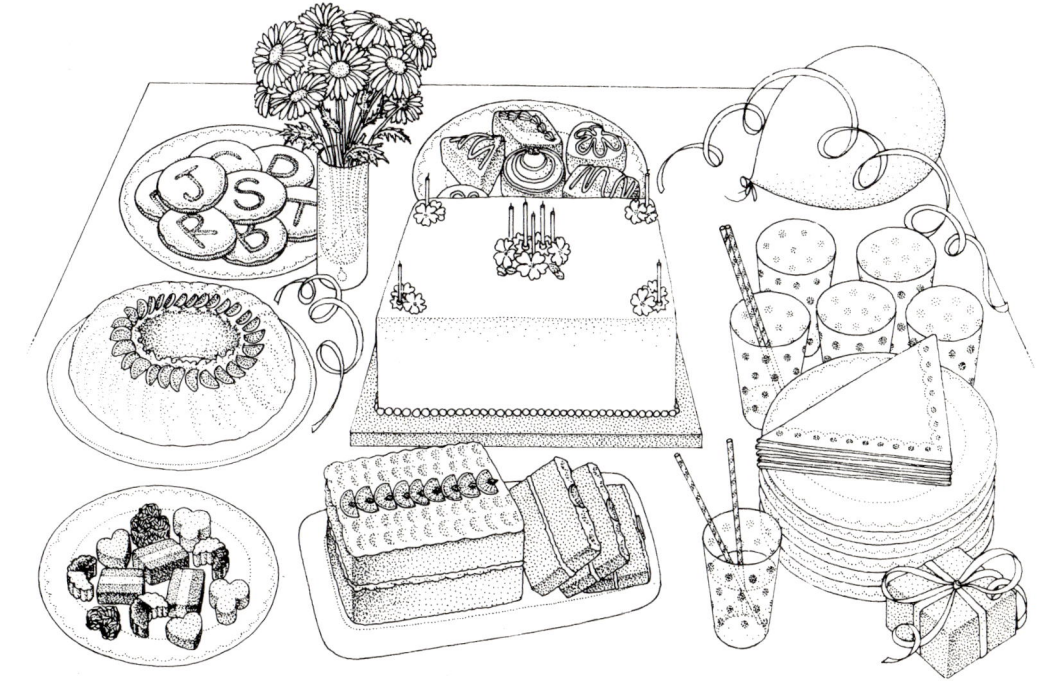

ICED CAKES FOR ALL OCCASIONS

TEATIME CAKES

Quick lacy sponge

This is the quickest and easiest method of decorating a cake, and is very effective on a teatime sponge if you haven't time to make icing.

You can use a paper doily, as here, or you can cut your own paper pattern and place it on the cake. Even a wire rack held over the cake will leave a delicate design in icing sugar.

2 Basic one-stage sandwich cakes (page 21)
4 tablespoons strawberry jam
1–2 tablespoons icing sugar

Sandwich the cakes together with the strawberry jam. Stand the cake on a wire rack and arrange a pretty, open-patterned doily on the surface. Using a dredger or a fine sieve, sprinkle icing sugar over the doily, covering the cake top [1]. Lift away the doily to leave the sugar pattern underneath [2].

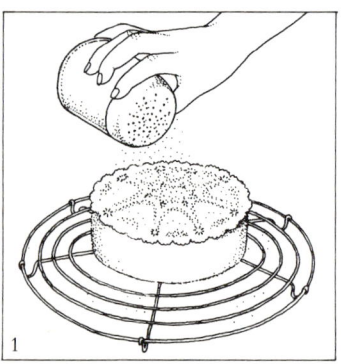
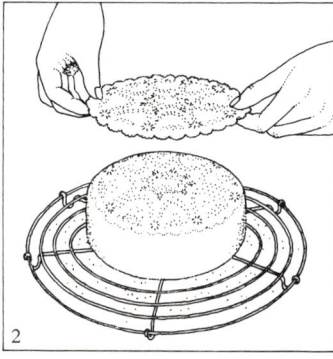

Glacé-iced sponge (page 60)
Lattice sponge (page 60)
Orange feather-iced cake (page 61)

Glacé-iced sponge

Illustrated on page 59

After the Quick lacy sponge (see page 58), the next simplest way of icing a cake is with glacé icing. For a quick tea-time treat, simply flood the cake with glacé icing and decorate it, if you like, with whatever you have in your store cupboard – hundreds and thousands, chocolate vermicelli, mimosa balls, toasted coconut.

2 Basic one-stage sandwich cakes (page 21)
4 tablespoons strawberry jam
½ quantity Glacé icing (page 29)
4 tablespoons long thread coconut

Sandwich the cakes together with the strawberry jam. Place the cake on a plate and flood the top with glacé icing, spreading evenly to the edge. If any icing runs over the edge, leave it to dry and remove it carefully with a sharp knife. Allow the icing to set.

Place the coconut on a baking tray and toast it lightly under the grill, stirring from time to time, until golden brown. Sprinkle it evenly around the edge of the icing to decorate.

Lattice sponge

Illustrated on page 59

If you have more time to spare you can add to the cake by piping different coloured glacé icing over the top. Be very careful when using food colourings, though; a very little can produce quite a strong result. It's best to beat the colouring in, one drop at a time, until the desired shade is reached.

2 Basic one-stage sandwich cakes (page 21)
4 tablespoons apricot jam
1 quantity Glacé icing (page 29)
green food colouring
angelica

Sandwich the cakes together with the apricot jam as before and place the cake on a wire rack. Reserve about 2 tablespoons glacé icing on one side and pour the rest on to the cake, spreading it all over with a palette knife, as shown [1]. Leave to dry.

Colour the reserved glacé icing pale green and place it in a greaseproof icing bag. Snip the tip off the bag and pipe parallel lines, about 2.5 cm/1 in apart, over the cake [2]. Turn the cake and pipe more lines at right angles to the first set, to give a lattice design [3].

Cut 8 diamond shapes out of the angelica and arrange these in pairs around the edge of the cake to decorate.

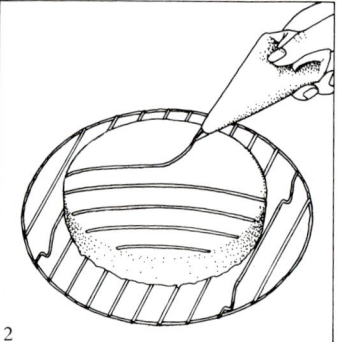

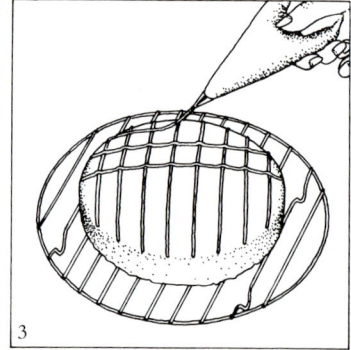

Orange feather-iced sandwich cake

Illustrated on page 59

The feather-icing technique explained in Basic Techniques (see page 37) can be adapted, as here, to create all sorts of patterns. By piping lines in unusual ways or using different colours you can easily make up your own designs.

2 Orange-flavoured Victoria or one-stage sandwich cakes (page 21)
4 tablespoons orange marmalade
1 quantity Glacé icing (page 29)
orange food colouring

Sandwich the cakes together with the marmalade and place on a plate. Put 2–3 tablespoons of the glacé icing in a grease-proof piping bag without a nozzle and leave on one side. Colour the rest a rich orange. Pour the orange icing over the cake and spread it quickly and evenly with a palette knife almost to the edge.

Snip off the very tip of the piping bag and, working quickly before the icing has a chance to set, pipe a spiral of white icing on top of the orange, running from the centre of the cake out towards the edge [1]. Now dip a skewer or the tip of a knife briefly into water and draw it across the spiral, from the centre of the cake straight out to the edge. Continue drawing more lines an equal distance apart [2] until you have covered the cake, dipping your skewer or knife into water every so often to give a clean, smooth result. Allow the icing to dry before serving.

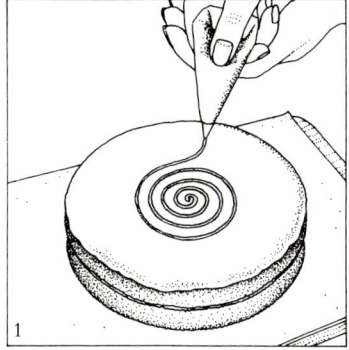
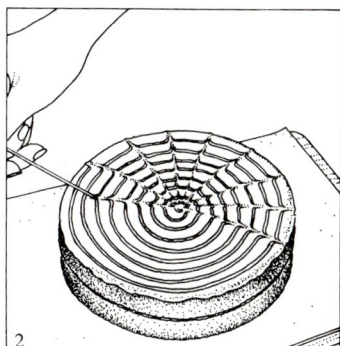

Teatime fruit ring

Illustrated on page 10

1 quantity Light fruit cake mixture (page 24), using sultanas only instead of mixed dried fruit
1 quantity Lemon glacé icing (page 29)
a few crystallised grapes to decorate (page 52)

Set the oven at moderate (170 C, 325 F, gas 3). Grease and flour a 1.75-litre (3-pint) ring tin and fill it with the cake mixture. Bake for 1 hour until well risen and golden and a skewer inserted into the cake comes out clean. Cool for a few minutes in the tin before turning the cake out and allowing it to cool completely on a wire rack.

When cold, spoon the glacé icing over the ring with a tablespoon so that it drizzles down the side, as shown. Do this while the cake is still on the wire rack rather than on a plate; any icing that drizzles through the rack on to your work surface can easily be wiped away later.

Place the grapes in small clusters around the top of the cake to decorate. Leave the icing to dry before transferring the cake to a plate.

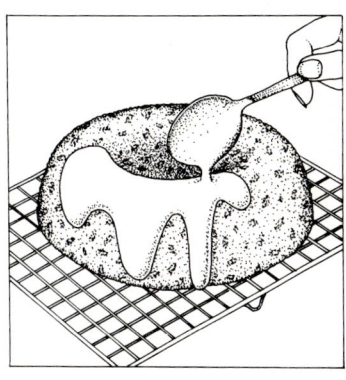

ICED CAKES FOR ALL OCCASIONS

Lemon fudge loaf

1½ quantities Lemon-flavoured Victoria sandwich mixture (page 21)
1 quantity Lemon fudge icing (page 29)
5 crystallised fresh lemon slices, halved (see below)
angelica

Set the oven at moderate (180 C, 350 F, gas 4). Grease and line the base of a 900-g/2-lb loaf tin and turn the cake mixture into it. Bake for about 45 minutes until golden and firm, then turn out and cool on a wire rack. Split the cake horizontally into three and sandwich back together, using two thirds of the fudge icing.
  Spread the remaining icing on top of the cake and, using the tip of a palette knife, press four lines of half-moon shapes in the surface, as shown, leaving a smooth strip down the centre. Decorate with the lemon slices and angelica.

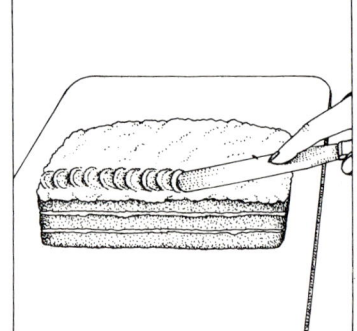

CRYSTALLISED LEMON SLICES

50 g/2 oz caster sugar
3 tablespoons water
5 fresh lemon slices

Heat the sugar and water gently in a pan until the sugar has dissolved. Bring to the boil and add the lemon slices. Simmer gently for about 5 minutes, turning the slices occasionally, then lift them out and place them on a cooling rack. Allow the slices to dry for at least 30 minutes before cutting them in half.

Lemon sunflower (page 64)
Frosted caramel roll (page 65)

Lemon sunflower

Illustrated on page 63

A flower-shaped cake lends itself well to different ways of icing: this sunflower will make a delightful centrepiece for your tea table. Drawing smooth, evenly rounded petals needs a steady hand, so if you're not sure of yourself, it's a good idea to practise on the tin first.

Double quantity Lemon-flavoured Victoria sandwich mixture (page 21)
50 g/2 oz flaked almonds
¾ quantity Lemon butter cream (page 28)
½ quantity Lemon glacé icing (page 29)
yellow food colouring
1 teaspoon chocolate vermicelli

Set the oven at moderate (180 C, 350 F, gas 4). Lightly grease and line the base of a 2.5-litre (4½-pint) flower-shaped cake tin. Spoon the cake mixture into the tin and bake for 50 minutes until firm and golden. Turn out and cool on a wire rack.

Place the flaked almonds in a shallow baking tin or flame-proof dish and toast gently under the grill for a few moments, stirring occasionally, until golden brown.

Spread the butter cream round the sides of the cooled cake. Cover the butter cream with the almonds by pressing the almonds on to the sides with the aid of a palette knife, as shown [**1**]. Carefully transfer the cake to a plate.

Colour the glacé icing yellow and place about 2 tablespoons of it in a piping bag fitted with a No. 2 plain writing nozzle. Pipe a small circle in the centre of the cake and follow this by piping the outlines of the petals, each joined to the centre of the flower, as shown [**2**].

Flood the petals and centre of the flower with the remaining glacé icing, easing it gently round the inside of the shapes with a skewer or a paint brush, [**3**], and making sure that you prick out any air bubbles. Sprinkle the chocolate vermicelli lightly in the centre of the flower while the icing is still wet. Allow the cake to dry.

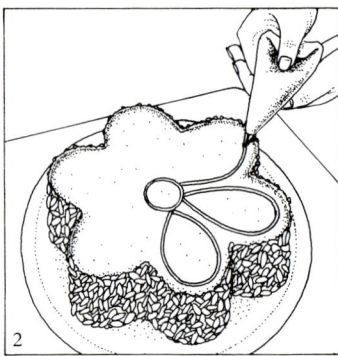
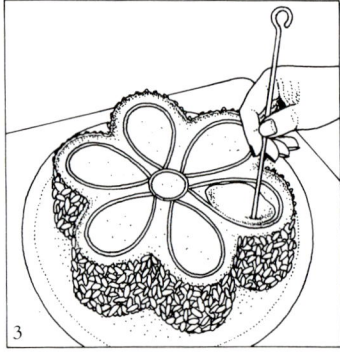

Frosted caramel roll

Illustrated on page 63

100 g/4 oz unsalted peanuts
150 g/5 oz caster sugar
1 quantity Caramel American frosting (page 30)
1 Swiss roll (page 23), rolled in greaseproof paper and cooled

Roughly chop the peanuts and place them in a heavy-based pan with the sugar. Allow the sugar to dissolve over a very low heat, without boiling. Shake the pan occasionally but do not stir. When the sugar has dissolved, boil the mixture rapidly until it turns a rich, golden caramel colour. Pour it into an oiled tin and allow to cool and set. When set, tap half the caramel with a hammer to break it into pieces and finely crush the remainder with a rolling pin.

Make the caramel frosting. Unroll the Swiss roll and spread it with about a quarter of the frosting; sprinkle the crushed nut caramel over the top, reroll and place it on a plate. Spread the remaining frosting all over the roll, peaking up with a fork, as shown. Decorate with the pieces of caramel and serve.

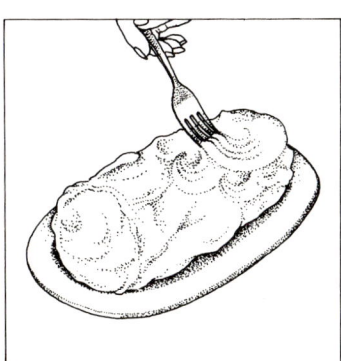

Citrus ring

Illustrated on page 67

1½ quantities Orange-flavoured Victoria sandwich mixture (page 21)
1 quantity Lemon 7-minute frosting (page 30)
small orange and lemon-flavoured jelly slices

Set the oven at moderate (160 C, 325 F, gas 3). Grease and flour a 1.4-litre (2½-pint) ring tin. Spoon the Victoria sandwich mixture into the tin and bake it for 40–45 minutes until golden and firm to the touch. Turn the cake out and leave it to cool on a wire rack.

Make the frosting. Place the cooled cake on a plate and cover it completely with the frosting. As you do so, turn the plate with one hand and guide the palette knife with the other over the frosting in an up-and-down motion, as shown, to give a swirled effect.

Decorate the ring with alternate orange and lemon slices and serve.

VARIATION

Instead of using bought orange and lemon jelly slices, you can decorate your Citrus ring with crystallised fresh orange and lemon slices (see page 62) or even fresh or drained canned mandarin segments.

A very attractive effect is created if you scatter fine curls of orange and lemon peel over the frosting.

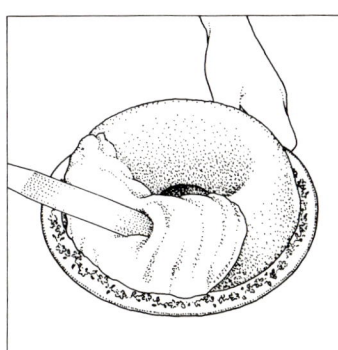

Coffee banana slice

1 quantity Coffee-flavoured Victoria sandwich mixture (page 21)
2 small bananas
a little lemon juice
¾ quantity Coffee butter cream (page 28)
chocolate coffee beans

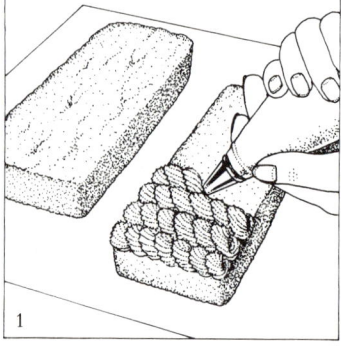

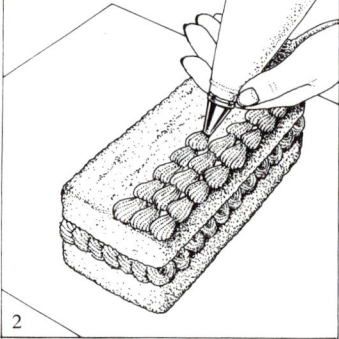

Set the oven at moderate (180 C, 350 F, gas 4). Grease and base-line a 450-g/1-lb loaf tin. Make the cake mixture in the usual way but just before turning it into the tin, mash one banana and stir it into the mixture. Bake for 35–40 minutes until golden and firm, turn out and cool on a wire rack.

Slice the remaining banana, dipping the slices in lemon juice to prevent discoloration. Place the butter cream in a piping bag fitted with a No. 8 star nozzle. Split the cake horizontally into two halves. Pipe about one third of the butter cream on the bottom half in continuous, swirling lines parallel with the shortest edge, as shown [**1**], and sandwich the two halves together. Pipe the remaining butter cream on top of the cake in lines of shell following the longest edge [**2**]. Decorate with the banana slices and chocolate coffee beans.

Citrus ring (page 65)
Chocolate peppermint swirl (page 68)
Lemon cup cakes (page 68)

Chocolate peppermint swirl

Illustrated on page 67

1 quantity Basic Victoria sandwich mixture (page 21)
1½ tablespoons cocoa powder
2 teaspoons hot water
a few drops peppermint essence
green food colouring
1 quantity 7-minute frosting (page 30)
chocolate-coated mint creams to decorate

Set the oven at moderate (180 C, 350 F, gas 4). Grease and base-line a 15-cm (6-in) round cake tin.

Divide the cake mixture into two equal portions. Dissolve the cocoa powder in the hot water and mix this well into one half; to the other half, add the peppermint essence and a little green food colouring. Drop the mixtures in alternate spoonfuls into the tin to give a marbled effect once the cake is baked. If you like, you can quickly drag a knife round the mixture in the tin to ensure that the colours run smoothly into each other.

Bake the cake for about 1 hour until firm to the touch and golden and beginning to come away from the side of the tin. Turn it out and leave to cool on a wire rack.

Make the frosting. Transfer the cake to a plate and cover it with the frosting, swirling in a circular motion with a palette knife, as shown. Cut the chocolate mint creams in half and arrange them, cut halves uppermost, around the frosting to decorate.

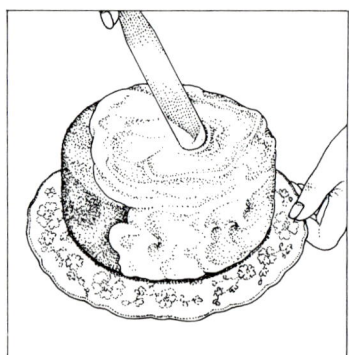

Lemon cup cakes

Illustrated on page 67

1 quantity Basic Victoria or one-stage sandwich mixture (page 21)
¾ quantity Lemon butter cream (page 28)
225 g/8 oz lemon curd

Set the oven at moderate (180 C, 350 F, gas 4). Place 18 paper cake cases in patty tins. Divide the cake mixture between the cases and bake for about 20 minutes or until golden and firm to the touch. Cool the cakes on a wire rack.

Place the butter cream in a piping bag fitted with a No. 8 star nozzle and pipe a ring of butter cream around the top of each cake, leaving the centre uncovered. Beat the lemon curd lightly until smooth and spoon it carefully on to the tops of the cakes, easing it gently around the inside of the butter cream.

GÂTEAUX

Black Forest gâteau

Illustrated on page 71

1 quantity Chocolate-flavoured whisked sponge mixture (page 22)
1 (425-g/15-oz) can black cherries
2 teaspoons arrowroot
2 tablespoons Kirsch liqueur
450 ml/¾ pint whipping cream
75 g/3 oz plain dessert chocolate, grated
75 g/3 oz chocolate caraque (page 50)
a little icing sugar
maraschino cherries to decorate

Set the oven at moderately hot (190 C, 375 F, gas 5). Grease and line a 23-cm (9-in) round cake tin and bake the cake in it for about 30 minutes. Turn out and cool on a wire rack, then slice horizontally into three.

Drain the juice from the cherries into a pan. Pour 1 tablespoon of this into a bowl and mix it with the arrowroot. Heat the rest of the juice almost to boiling point and pour it into the bowl, stirring until smooth. Return the mixture to the pan, bring to the boil and boil it for about 1 minute until it has become clear. Allow to cool.

Stone the cherries and add them to the thickened juice. Spread half the cherries on the bottom layer of cake and sprinkle them with 1 tablespoon Kirsch. Whip the cream until thick and spread a thin layer over the fruit. Repeat these layers, finishing with the third piece of sponge, and place the cake on a plate.

Spread a layer of cream around the side of the cake. Using a palette knife, press the grated chocolate lightly against it until the cake is coated all round. Spread more cream on top of the cake and decorate with lines of chocolate caraque. Sprinkle with icing sugar.

Place all the remaining cream in a piping bag fitted with a large vegetable nozzle and pipe a rosette at the end of each line of caraque. Top with the maraschino cherries.

Chocolate rum sandwich

Illustrated on page 71

1 quantity Chocolate butter cream, made with rum instead of milk (page 28)
2 Chocolate-flavoured Victoria or one-stage sandwich cakes (page 21)
¾ quantity Chocolate glacé icing (page 29)
10–14 chocolate leaves (page 51)

Use about one fifth of the butter cream to sandwich the cakes together and place the cake on a sheet of greaseproof paper. Spread half the remaining butter cream over the side of the cake in a thin, even layer and draw a serrated icing comb round it for a ribbed effect. Place the gâteau on a plate.

Transfer the remaining butter cream to a piping bag fitted with a No. 8 star nozzle and pipe a shell border around the top edge of the cake. Flood the centre with the glacé icing, taking it right up to the butter cream border and pricking out all air bubbles with a skewer or palette knife. Allow to set. Decorate with the chocolate leaves.

Pineapple ginger slice

1 quantity Basic whisked sponge mixture (page 22)
150 g/5 oz Apricot glaze (page 30)
300 ml/½ pint double cream
1 tablespoon ginger wine
1 (227-g/8-oz) can pineapple rings, drained and chopped
15 g/½ oz crystallised ginger, chopped

Set the oven at moderately hot (190 C, 375 F, gas 5). Grease and flour a 900-g (2-lb) loaf tin and line the base. Turn the cake mixture into the tin and bake for 20–25 mins until well risen and golden. Turn out and cool on a wire rack.

Split the cooled cake in half horizontally and brush the top and sides of one half with apricot glaze. Whip the cream until thick and whip in the ginger wine. Spread about one third of the cream over the glazed half of the cake and sprinkle with the pineapple.

Brush the sides of the remaining piece of cake with apricot glaze and place it on the pineapple. Spread a thin layer of cream over the top.

Place the remaining apricot glaze in a greaseproof piping bag, snip off the tip and pipe lines across the cream. Draw a skewer across the lines in the opposite direction to feather ice.

Using a large star vegetable nozzle, pipe the rest of the cream in a shell border around the top of the cake. Decorate with the ginger.

Black Forest gâteau (page 69)
Chocolate rum sandwich (page 69)
Iced chocolate square (page 72)

Coffee walnut gâteau

Illustrated on the front cover

2 Genoese sponge cakes (page 22)
1¼ quantities Coffee crème au beurre (page 28)
50 g/2 oz finely chopped walnuts
walnut halves to decorate

Sandwich the cakes together with one third of the crème au beurre.

Use a third of the remaining crème au beurre to coat the side of the cake, smoothing with a palette knife. Sprinkle the chopped walnuts on a sheet of greaseproof paper, stand the cake on its side and, steadying it with your hands (see page 38), roll the cake along the nuts until the side is completely coated.

Place the cake on a plate. Spread half the remaining crème au beurre on top of the cake and draw the flat of your palette knife across it from side to side in long, sweeping movements to decorate, as shown [1]. Place the rest of the crème au beurre in a piping bag fitted with a large star-shaped vegetable nozzle and pipe a shell border around the edge [2]. Pipe a swirl in the centre and decorate the cake with walnut halves.

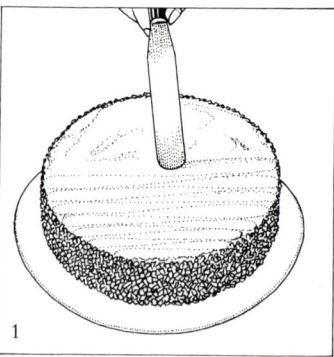
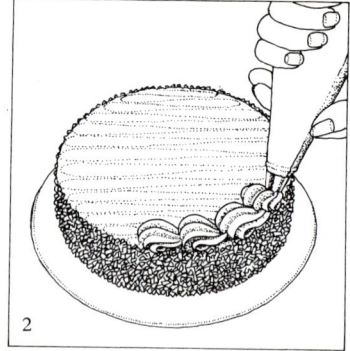

Iced chocolate square

Illustrated on page 71

1 quantity Chocolate-flavoured Victoria sandwich mixture (page 21)
1 quantity Vanilla butter cream (page 28)
175 g/6 oz cooking or plain dessert chocolate

Set the oven at moderate (180 C, 350 F, gas 4). Grease and line a 15-cm (6-in) square cake tin. Bake the cake mixture in this for 40–45 minutes until firm; turn out and cool on a wire rack.

Split the cake horizontally into two and sandwich together with half the butter cream. Spread the remaining butter cream around the sides and draw a serrated icing comb straight along each side for a ribbed effect.

Melt half the chocolate and spread it on to non-stick paper. When almost set, use a ruler to mark off 20 (2.5-cm/1-in) squares [1] and cut them out [2]. Cut eight of the squares in half to form 16 triangles.

Melt the remaining chocolate and pour it over the top of the cake. Just as the chocolate is beginning to set, draw the serrated icing comb across it in a zig-zag pattern. Finish the cake by sticking three chocolate squares flat into the butter cream on each side and four triangles along each top edge in the setting chocolate, pointing out from the cake.

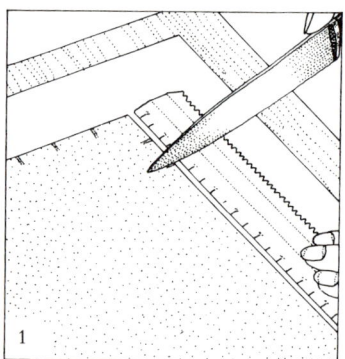
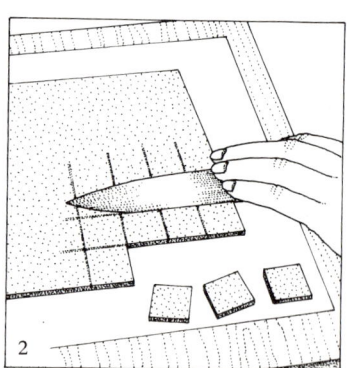

CELEBRATION CAKES

Numeral birthday cake

Illustrated on page 75

1½ quantities Basic Victoria sandwich mixture (page 21)
double quantity Butter cream (page 28)
food colourings
50 g/2 oz Almond paste (page 31)
pink candles and candle holders

Set the oven at moderate (160 C, 325 F, gas 3). Grease and base-line a 1.75-litre (3-pint) numeral-shaped tin and bake the cake mixture in it for 30–35 minutes. Turn out and cool on a wire rack.

Place the cake on a plate or board. Cover it with about three quarters of the butter cream, swirling a pattern with a palette knife. Colour the remaining butter icing pink and place it in a piping bag fitted with a No. 8 star nozzle. Pipe a star border around the top edge of the cake [**1**], then around the bottom.

Colour the almond paste pink and mould it into a small mouse, with a long tail, ears and a pointed nose [**2**]. Arrange it on the cake with the candles. Paint eyes and whiskers with black food colouring.

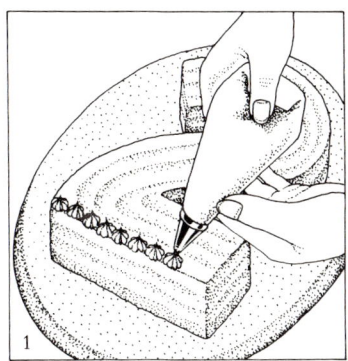
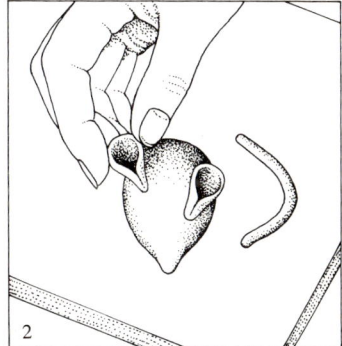

Primrose birthday cake

Illustrated on page 75

1 (18-cm/7-in) square Light fruit cake (page 24)
Apricot glaze (page 30)
675 g/1½ lb Almond paste (page 31)
1 quantity Boiled fondant icing (page 33)
yellow food colouring
1 (23-cm/9-in) square cake board
crystallised primroses (page 52)
yellow candles with holders

Brush the cake with apricot glaze and cover it with the almond paste. Allow to dry for a few days.

Warm about four fifths of the fondant to a pouring temperature (see page 34), colour it a pale primrose yellow and pour it over the cake, coating evenly on all sides. Allow to dry for 1 hour.

Fix the cake to the board with a dab of jam. Warm the remaining fondant to a piping consistency (see page 34), and colour it pale yellow. Using a No. 3 plain nozzle, pipe a border of dots all around the bottom edge of the cake and allow to dry. Arrange the candles on the cake and surround them with crystallised primroses.

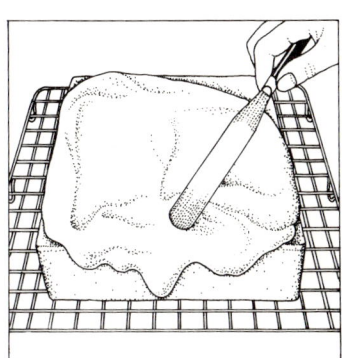

ICED CAKES FOR ALL OCCASIONS

Eighteenth birthday cake

1¼ quantities Genoese cake mixture (page 22)
double quantity Crème au beurre (page 28)
blue and green food colourings
1 (28-cm/11-in) round cake board
silver sugar balls
1 (5-cm/2-in) silver Eighteenth birthday key

Set the oven at moderately hot (190 C, 375 F, gas 5). Grease and line a 23-cm (9-in) round tin and bake the cake mixture in it for 40–45 minutes until firm. Turn out and cool on a wire rack, then slice in half horizontally and sandwich back together with a quarter of the crème au beurre.

Colour about three quarters of the remaining crème au beurre turquoise blue, using blue and green food colourings. Place the cake on the board and cover it with turquoise icing. Run a serrated icing comb around the side and, using a palette knife, draw curved swirls on the top from the centre out to the edge.

Place the plain crème au beurre in a piping bag fitted with a No. 18 petal nozzle. Holding the nozzle at an angle to the surface of the cake, pipe a zig-zag border first round the top, then round the bottom edge, as shown. Using the same nozzle, pipe small daisies (see page 45) at intervals on the side of the cake and place a silver ball in the centre of each. Top the cake with the key.

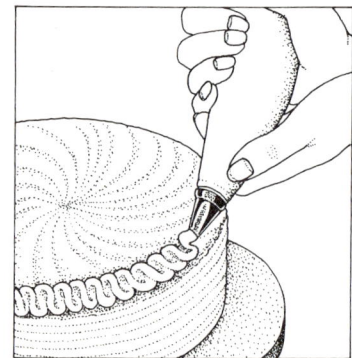

Primrose birthday cake (page 73)
Numeral birthday cake (page 73)

Buttercup birthday cake

Illustrated on the front cover

1 (20-cm/8-in) square Rich fruit cake (pages 24–25)
Apricot glaze (page 30)
1 quantity Almond paste (page 31)
1 (25-cm/10-in) square cake board
1½ quantities Royal icing (page 32)
yellow and green food colourings
narrow yellow satin ribbon

Brush the cake all over with apricot glaze, cover it with almond paste and allow to dry for about a week. Position the cake on the board and fix it with a dab of icing. Flat ice the cake with two thirds of the royal icing, taking the icing to the edge of the board. Leave the cake to dry for 48 hours after applying the last coat.

Meanwhile colour all but 3 tablespoons of the remaining icing a bright buttercup yellow. Beat in a little more icing sugar to give it a piping consistency and place about half of it in an icing bag fitted with a No. 18 petal nozzle. (Keep the remainder stored in an airtight container in the refrigerator until you need it.) Fix a piece of non-stick or greaseproof paper on top of an icing nail and, holding the nozzle at an angle of 45° to the surface of the nail, pipe five rounded, slightly overlapping petals to make a buttercup [1]. Remove the paper and allow the buttercup to dry while you pipe the next one. Continue in this way, piping about 30 buttercups in all, and allow them to dry for 24 hours.

To decorate the cake, place all the remaining yellow icing in a piping bag fitted with a No. 2 plain writing nozzle. Make a template (see page 42) for the birthday message you wish to write and lightly mark the outline on the cake with a pin. Pipe round the outline [2]. Alternatively, if you feel confident, pipe the message freehand directly on to the cake.

Pipe a border of small loops running just below the top edge of the cake and match this with a border all along the bottom edge, as shown [3]. Change to a No. 1 plain writing nozzle and pipe tiny dots in the centre of each dried buttercup for the stamens. Remove the buttercups from the pieces of non-stick paper and arrange them in groups in the corners on the top of the cake and around the board, securing each buttercup with a dab of icing.

Colour the reserved 3 tablespoons royal icing a bright, leafy green and place it in a bag fitted with a No. 2 plain writing nozzle. Pipe tiny leaves pointing outwards from the buttercups by holding the nozzle almost flat against the surface of the cake and piping continuous, overlapping spirals, beginning wide and tapering to a point [4].

Allow all the icing to dry, then tie the ribbon round the sides with a soft bow.

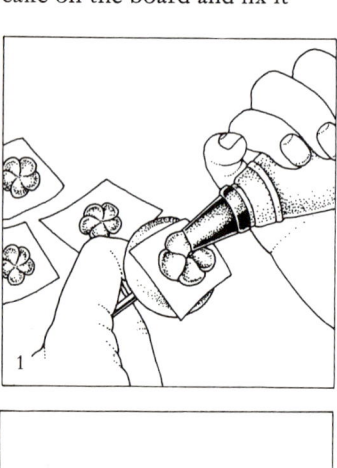
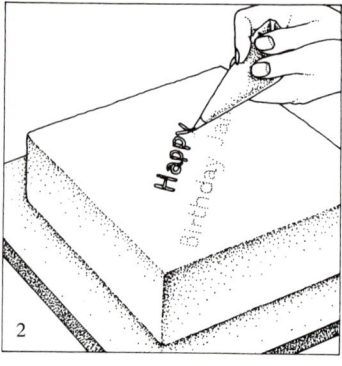
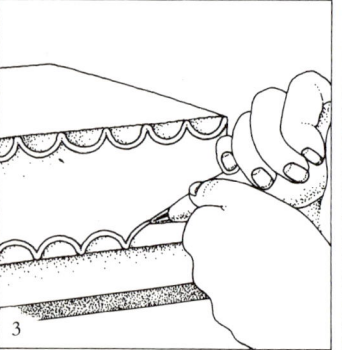
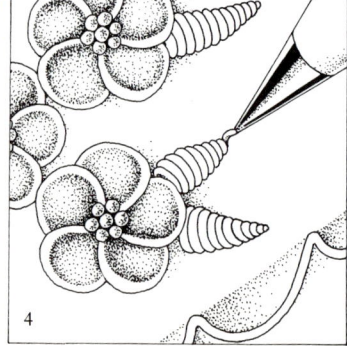

Strawberry Valentine cake

Illustrated on pages 78–9

1 quantity Genoese sponge mixture (page 22)
1½ quantities Strawberry crème au beurre (page 28)
175 g/6 oz fresh strawberries
1 (25-cm/10-in) heart-shaped or round cake board
75 g/3 oz plain dessert chocolate

Set the oven at moderately hot (190 C, 375 F, gas 5). Grease and base-line a 1.15-litre (2-pint) heart-shaped tin and bake the cake mixture in it for 20–25 minutes. Turn out and cool on a wire rack.

Divide the crème au beurre into four equal portions. Slice the cake in half horizontally and spread one portion over the bottom half. Reserve two strawberries for decoration and roughly chop the rest. Arrange the chopped strawberries over the layer of crème au beurre and sandwich the two halves together. Place the cake on the board. Spread the top and sides of the cake with two more portions of crème au beurre, swirling in circles with a palette knife.

Melt the chocolate and dip each reserved strawberry into it until half-coated [1]; leave to dry. Pour the remaining chocolate on a sheet of waxed or non-stick paper and allow to cool. Cut out small hearts with a heart-shaped aspic cutter.

Place the remaining crème au beurre in a piping bag fitted with a No. 12 shell nozzle and pipe a border of shell around the top edge of the cake [2].

Decorate with the strawberries and chocolate hearts.

Note If fresh strawberries are difficult to obtain, substitute frozen ones. Or try using fresh grapes instead.

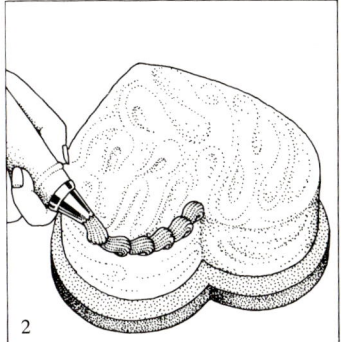

Mother's Day cake

Illustrated on pages 78–79

2 Basic whisked sponge cakes (page 22)
4 tablespoons black cherry jam
1 quantity Boiled fondant icing (page 33)
lilac food colouring
1 (2.5-cm/1-in wide) pink ribbon
crystallised pink rose buds and leaves (page 52)

Sandwich the cakes together with the jam. Reserve about 4 tablespoons fondant on one side and warm the rest with some stock syrup to a pouring consistency (see page 34). Colour it pale lilac. Place the cake on a wire rack and pour the fondant over it to coat as smoothly as possible. Allow to dry for at least 1 hour, then carefully transfer the cake to a plate or cake board.

Heat the reserved fondant gently with a little stock syrup to a piping consistency (see page 34) and transfer it to a piping bag fitted with a No. 8 star or a No. 12 shell nozzle. Pipe a border of small shells around the bottom edge of the cake, where the cake meets the plate or board. Allow to dry. Tie the ribbon round the side of the cake and arrange the roses and leaves on the top.

Overleaf: Mother's Day cake
Strawberry Valentine cake
Easter cake (page 80)
Simnel cake (page 81)

Iced cakes for all occasions

Easter cake

Illustrated on pages 78–79

1 quantity Boiled or Kneaded
   fondant icing (pages 33–34)
yellow food colouring
1 (20-cm/8-in) square Farmhouse fruit cake (page 26)
Apricot glaze (page 30)
1 quantity Glacé icing (page 29)
yellow satin ribbon

Knead the fondant icing until smooth and easy to handle and work in enough yellow food colouring to give it a fairly bright yellow colour. Take a small amount of fondant and use it to mould three daffodils: for each one, cut out six petal shapes and a long strip to make the trumpet. Mould the strip round your finger into a tube, seal the join and press one end together to form the base of the trumpet. Moisten this slightly and arrange the petals around it in a flower shape [**1**]. Leave the daffodils to dry.

Use some more fondant to mould Easter bunnies. For each bunny mould one ball for the body and a slightly smaller one for the head. Mould two long ears and a round tail and assemble the bunnies, as shown [**2**]. Leave them on one side to firm up while you finish the cake.

Use the remaining fondant to make four plaits to fit round the top of the cake. Divide the fondant into four portions; out of each portion roll three 23-cm (9-in) long, thin ropes and plait them loosely together [**3**]. Fit the plaits around the top edges of the cake, brushing the cake with apricot glaze before laying them down to fix them in place [**4**]. Reserve about 2 tablespoons of glacé icing and use the rest to flood the top of the cake, taking the icing right up to the plaited border. Allow to dry.

Place the reserved glacé icing in a piping bag fitted with a No. 1 or 2 plain writing nozzle and pipe eyes, nose and whiskers on the rabbits' faces. Finish by brushing a little icing on their tails. Arrange one daffodil in each of the three corners of the cake and place the bunnies in the fourth. Tie the ribbon around the cake and serve.

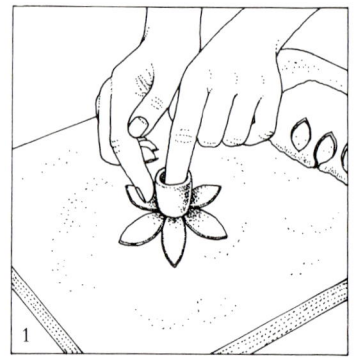

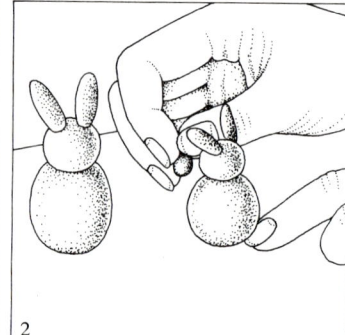

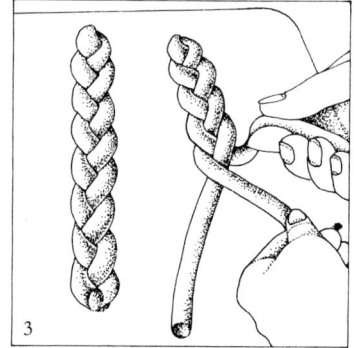

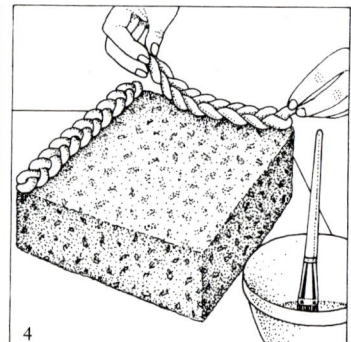

Simnel cake

Illustrated on pages 78–79

Rich fruit cake mixture for an 18-cm/7-in round tin (pages 24–25)
575 g/1 lb 4 oz Almond paste (page 31)
Apricot glaze (page 30)
beaten egg white to glaze

Set the oven at cool (150 C, 300 F, gas 2). Grease and line the cake tin and place half the cake mixture in it. Roll out about 100 g (4 oz) of the almond paste to a round 18 cm (7 in) in diameter and lay it on top of the cake mixture in the tin. Cover with the remaining mixture, smooth the surface and place the cake in the oven. Bake it for 2–2¼ hours or until firm and a skewer inserted into the centre comes out clean. Leave the cake to cool in the tin for about 1 hour before turning it out on to a wire rack.

Brush the top of the cake with apricot glaze. Roll out about half the remaining almond paste to a round to fit the top of the cake. Place the round in position and roll firmly over it with a rolling pin to smooth.

Using a sharp knife, mark parallel lines over the almond paste in a criss-cross pattern to decorate, as shown [1]. With the remaining almond paste, mould 11 small balls and arrange them around the top edge of the cake [2]. Brush the almond paste all over with beaten egg white [3] and place the cake under a hot grill for the almond paste to brown. If the balls begin to brown before the centre, cover them lightly with foil.

VARIATION

Use some of the almond paste to model an Easter chick [4].

Take a piece of paste of about 50 g/2 oz and divide it in half. Roll one half into a ball; pinch together one side and pull it upwards to form a tail. Roll half the remainder into a small ball for the head and put it in place. Roll out the rest into two small cones, press them flat and mark feathers on them with a knife. Fix the wings on the sides of the bird. Pipe eyes in royal icing.

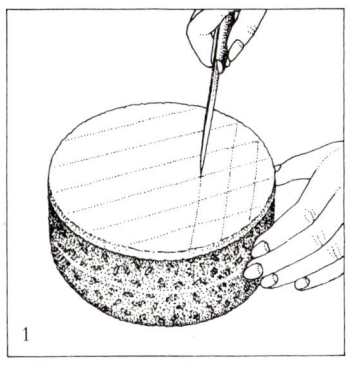

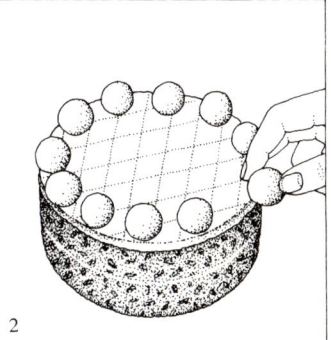

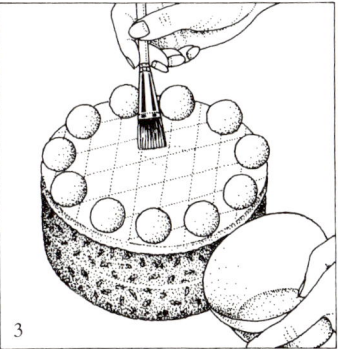

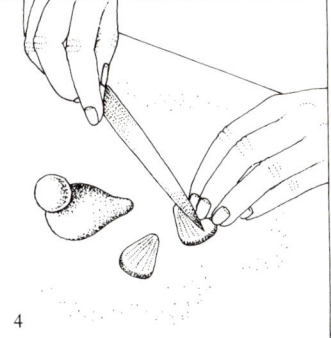

Harvest basket

1 quantity Farmhouse fruit cake mixture (page 26)
Apricot glaze (page 30)
1.5 kg/3½ lb Almond paste (page 31)
food colourings
1 (25-cm/10-in) square cake board
900 g/2 lb Royal icing (page 32)

Set the oven at moderate (170 C, 325 F, gas 3). Grease and line a 23 × 15 cm (9 × 6 in) rectangular cake tin and place the mixture in it. Bake the cake for about 1 hour 50 minutes or until a skewer inserted in the centre comes out clean. Allow to cool slightly in the tin, then turn out on to a wire rack.

When cool, brush the cake all over with apricot glaze and use about 900 g/2 lb of the almond paste to cover it. Leave the paste to dry out for about a week. Meanwhile use the remaining almond paste to make the handle and contents of the basket. For the handle, roll out three long, thick ropes of paste, plait them together and curve the plait into a crescent shape [**1**]. Model the rest of the almond paste into fruits (see page 48) and vegetables, working in food colourings where appropriate and using cloves for stalks. Paint a little brown food colouring on to the parsnips and carrots for traces of earth. Do the same to the potatoes, or roll them in chocolate powder, as shown [**2**]. Leave all the almond paste decorations to dry out for a few days.

Fix the cake to the board with a dab of royal icing. Colour the rest of the icing yellow to match the almond paste handle and spread a thin, even layer over the sides of the cake. Smooth the icing with an icing comb and allow to dry for 24 hours.

Divide the rest of the icing between two piping bags, one fitted with a No. 2 plain writing nozzle and the other with a basket nozzle. Use the plain nozzle to pipe parallel lines, about 1 cm (½ in) apart, down one side of the cake [**3**]. Change to the piping bag fitted with the basket nozzle and pipe a row of short lines, each about 2.5 cm (1 in) long, horizontally across the vertical lines so that every other vertical line is covered. Directly underneath this pipe another row with the basket nozzle, beginning about 1 cm (½ in) to the right of the first, giving a woven effect [**4**].

Finish the basket by piping a shell border all around the top edge, curving each shell slightly outwards, as shown, to give a twisted effect [**5**]. Allow all the icing to dry.

Before serving, attach the almond paste handle to the rim of the basket with a little royal icing and arrange all the fruits and vegetables on top.

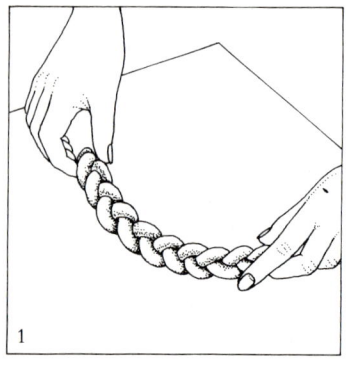

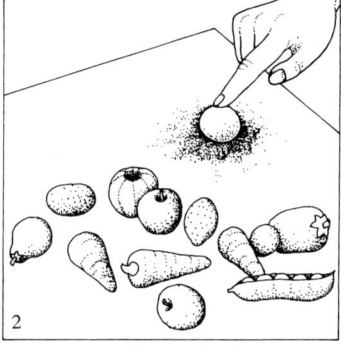

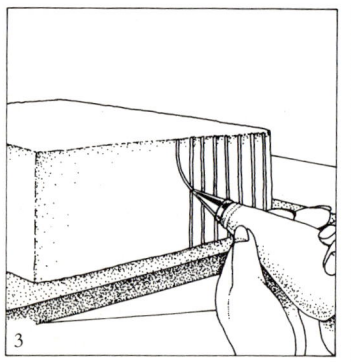

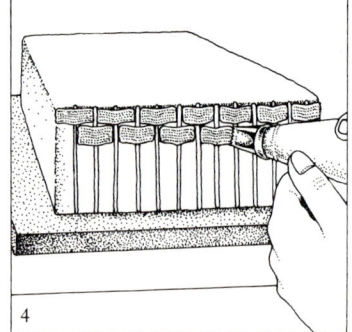

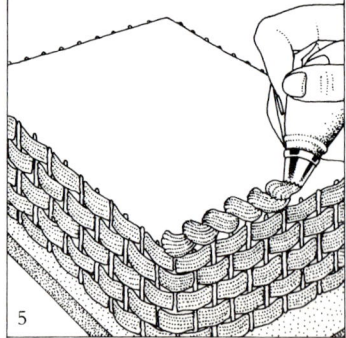

Light Christmas cake

Illustrated on page 6–7

1 (20-cm/8-in) round Light fruit cake (page 24)
Apricot glaze (page 30)
675 g/1½ lb Almond paste (page 31)
1 (23-cm/9-in) round cake board
1 quantity American frosting (page 30)
silver sugar balls
home-made almond paste decorations (pages 47–48) or bought Christmas cake decorations

Brush the cake all over with apricot glaze and cover it with the almond paste. Allow the paste to dry for a few days.

Position the cake on the board and fix it in place with a little of the American frosting. Use the rest of the frosting to cover the cake, pulling the icing up into rough peaks all over with the tip of a palette knife to give a snowy effect.

Allow the cake to dry for about 1 hour before scattering it with silver balls and arranging any Christmas decorations in the icing.

Chocolate yule log

Illustrated on page 87

1 Chocolate-flavoured Swiss roll, (page 23), unfilled
1½ quantities Chocolate butter cream (page 28)
75 g/3 oz Almond paste (page 31)
red and green food colourings
icing sugar for sprinkling

Fill the Swiss roll with a third of the butter cream and place it on a plate. Put the remaining butter cream in a piping bag fitted with a No. 8 star nozzle or a large vegetable nozzle and pipe rings on either end of the Swiss roll [**1**]. Now pipe lines along the roll to resemble bark on the log [**2**] and small, flat spirals for knotholes [**3**].

Colour a little almond paste bright red and roll it into tiny balls for holly berries. Colour the rest leafy green and make four small holly leaves (see page 47). Cut the remaining paste into ivy leaves, either freehand [**4**] or using the template given here. Mark veins on the leaves with a knife.

Arrange all the leaves and berries on the log and sprinkle the whole lightly with icing sugar.

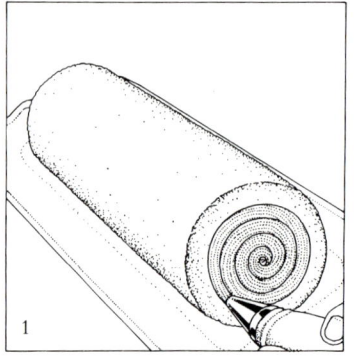
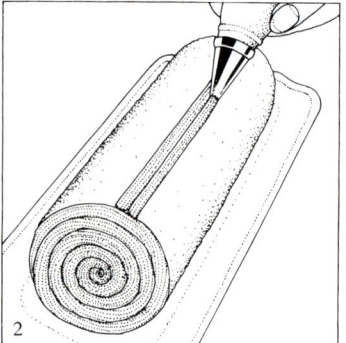
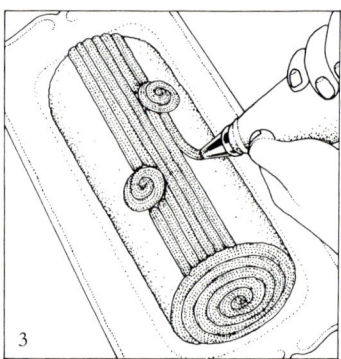
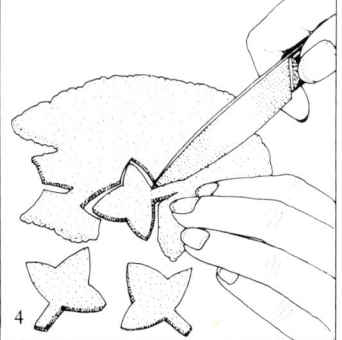

Christmas bell cake

Illustrated on page 87

1 (23-cm/9-in) round Rich fruit cake (pages 24–25)
Apricot glaze (page 30)
900 g/2 lb Almond paste (page 31)
1 (28-cm/11-in) round cake board
900 g/2 lb Royal icing (page 32)
½ teaspoon beaten egg white
3 tablespoons caster sugar
silver sugar balls
6 small plastic Christmas bells
white ribbon
small red candle

Brush the cake with apricot glaze and cover it with the almond paste. Allow the paste to dry out for a few days.

Fix the cake to the board with a dab of royal icing. Spread the rest of the icing all over the cake and pull it up into rough peaks around the side. On top, shape the icing into a swirling design with a palette knife [**1**]. Allow to dry for 24 hours.

Mix the egg white with the caster sugar, using a teaspoon, until the mixture just binds together (it will still be quite dry and crumbly). Spoon the mixture into the plastic Christmas bells, packing it in tightly. When all the bells are filled, gently tip them out on to non-stick paper [**2**]. The sugar should hold the bell shape. Leave the bells to dry for about 30 minutes or until the sugar is just drying around the edges. Now slip each sugar bell carefully back into its mould to hold it and scoop out the centres with a sharp knife [**3**]. Tip the bells out again and leave them for a few hours to dry completely. When dry, secure a silver ball inside each with a little royal icing [**4**].

Fix the candle in the centre of the cake with a dab of icing and arrange the white ribbon around it. Decorate the ribbon with the sugar bells.

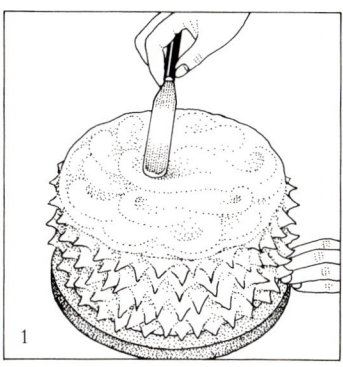

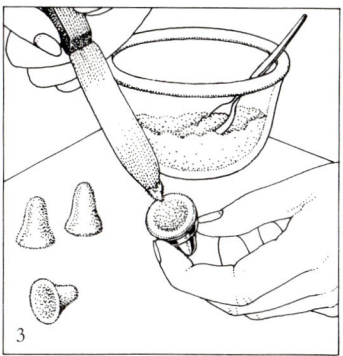

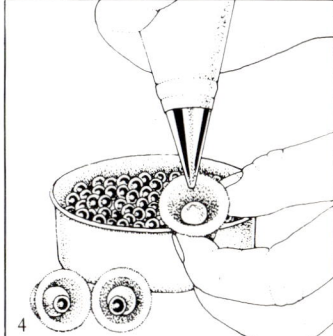

Snowman Christmas cake

Illustrated opposite

1 (23-cm/9-in) round Farm-
    house fruit cake (page 26)
Apricot glaze (page 30)
900 g/2 lb Almond paste
    (page 31)
1 (25-cm/10-in) round cake
    board
a little Royal icing (page 32)
1½ quantities Kneaded fondant
    icing (page 34)
food colourings
red satin ribbon

Brush the cake with apricot glaze and cover it with the almond paste. Allow to dry for a few days, then fix it to the board with a dab of royal icing. Roll out about one third of the fondant on a surface dusted with icing sugar or cornflour to a 30-cm (12-in) round. Lift it on to the cake with a rolling pin to prevent it tearing [1]. Dust your fingers with cornflour or icing sugar and quickly smooth the icing over the cake, moulding it round the shape and gently easing it down the side until both top and side are covered [2]. Rub your fingers over the fondant as you mould it to give a smooth, shiny texture. Trim surplus icing at the base [3] and leave to dry for 24 hours.

Use the remaining fondant to make the decorations. For the large snowman, roll one piece of fondant to a ball for the body and a smaller piece to a ball for the head. Model two small rolls for arms. Colour a little fondant green and mould it into a tiny cube and band: put these together to make a top hat. Colour some fondant red and roll it out to make a scarf. Assemble the snowman as shown [4], pressing the arms on to the body. Finish with a tiny carrot nose made from orange-coloured fondant. Using black or brown food colouring, paint eyes, mouth and buttons on the snowman and leave it to dry.

Make four smaller snowmen in the same way for the side of the cake but pressing their backs to make them flat [5].

Colour some of the remaining fondant green and some red and use it to make very small holly leaves (see pages 47–48) and berries. Allow all the decorations to dry for 24 hours.

Attach the ribbon round the cake, securing at the back with a pin. Fix the small snowmen at intervals on the ribbon with a little royal icing and place the larger snowman on top of the cake. Stick the holly leaves and berries around the snowmen with royal icing.

Christmas bell cake (page 85)
Snowman Christmas cake (above)
Chocolate yule log (page 84)

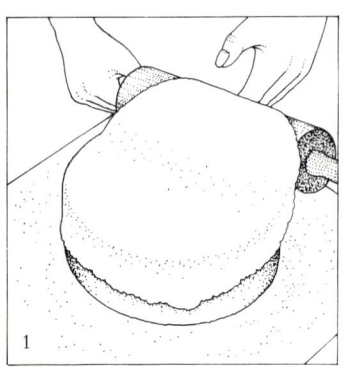
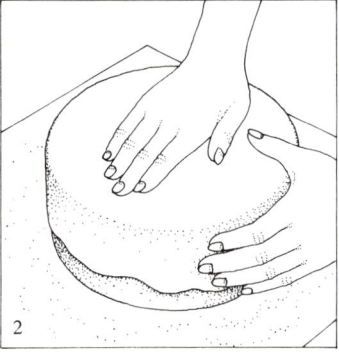
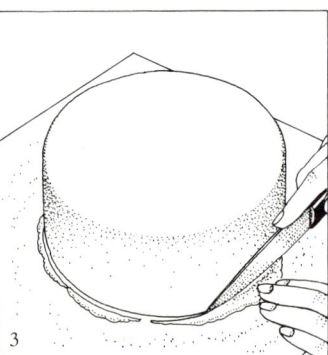
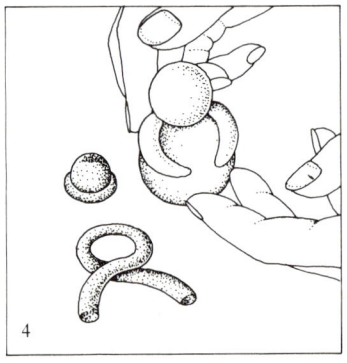
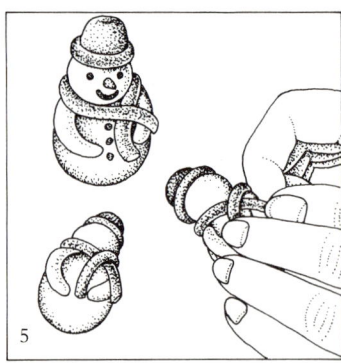

Robin redbreast Christmas cake

Illustrated on page 91

1 (23-cm/9-in) square Rich fruit cake (pages 24–25)
Apricot glaze (page 30)
1.25 kg/2½ lb Almond paste (page 31)
1 (28-cm/11-in) square cake board
1.5 kg/3¼ lb Royal icing (page 32)
food colourings

Brush the cake with apricot glaze and cover it with the almond paste. Allow it to dry for a week. Secure the cake to the board with a dab of royal icing and use all but 900 g/1 lb of the icing to flat ice the cake. Put it aside after applying the second coat and allow the cake to dry out for 48 hours.

Make the robin redbreast run-out (see page 46) using the template given here: trace the outline on to a piece of card and cover it with a sheet of waxed or non-stick paper. Using a No. 2 plain writing nozzle, pipe round the outline with white royal icing [**1**]. Thin down a little icing with water or egg white to a flooding consistency, colour it red or brown as appropriate and fill in the run-out, as shown [**2**], with a skewer or a fine paintbrush. Lift the paper holding the run-out carefully away from the card and leave the robin to dry in a warm, dry place for 2–3 days.

Make 32 holly leaf run-outs

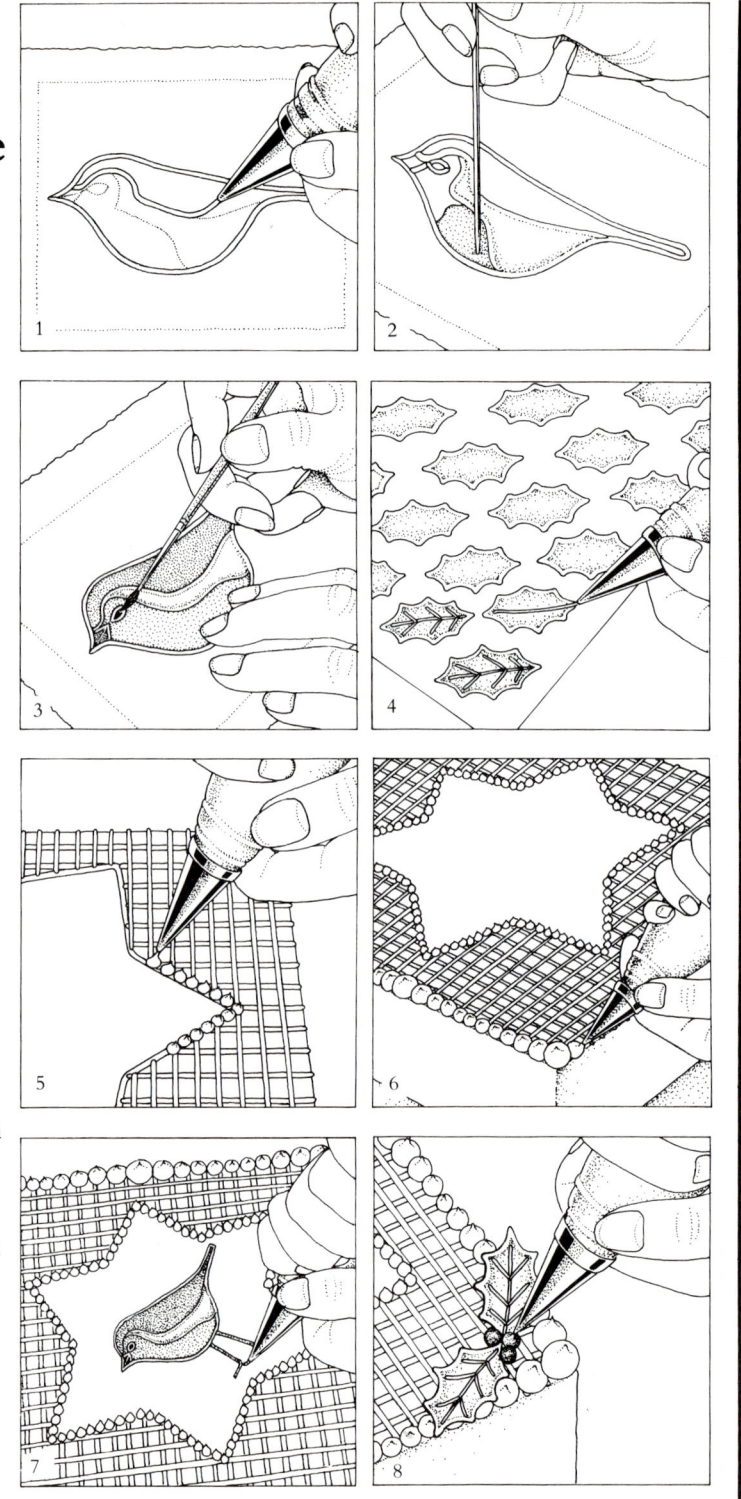

in the same way, using the template given here, together with a few extra ones in case you are unlucky enough to break some. Leave them to dry.

Using black and brown food colouring, watered down if necessary, paint the details of the beak, eye and feathers on the robin [3]. Using white royal icing and a No. 1 plain writing nozzle, pipe the pattern of the veins on the holly leaves, as shown [4]. Set aside to allow the icing to dry.

Make a large, star-shaped template (see page 42) and mark the outline of the star on top of the cake with a pin. Pipe round the star shape in white royal icing with a No. 2 plain writing nozzle. Using the same nozzle, fill the whole of the top of the cake outside the star shape with trellis work (see page 44).

Now pipe small adjoining dots all along the outline of the star shape, as shown [5]. Pipe more dots all along the top edge of the cake, making them larger as you get towards the corners and the middle of each side, as shown [6]. Do the same at the bottom edge of the cake along the line where it meets the board. Allow the icing to dry for a few hours.

Carefully slide the dried run-outs from the non-stick paper. Position the robin in the centre of the star and fix it in place with a dab of icing. Using brown icing and a No. 2 plain writing nozzle, pipe legs and feet on to the body of the robin [7]. Attach the holly leaves in pairs around the sides of the cake and on each corner with a little icing. Colour any remaining icing bright red and pipe red dots between the leaves to represent the holly berries [8].

The Christmas theme lends itself to many decorative variations. It's not hard to devise a template for a Christmas tree, or even a diminutive Father Christmas, or to draw the outline of a Christmas cracker. We have given some designs for you to choose from on pages 53–56, but greetings cards, magazines and illustrated books are all good sources of ideas. If you're very skilful you could perhaps create a row of carol singers, complete with books and candles. The design possibilities are endless, for once you have constructed your template, the principles of the techniques are the same, whatever shape you wish to reproduce.

And, of course, you can simply repeat the design in reverse. Two robins facing each other, or perhaps additional pairs of holly leaves at the points of the star are other possibilities for varying this particular design.

Poinsettia Christmas cake

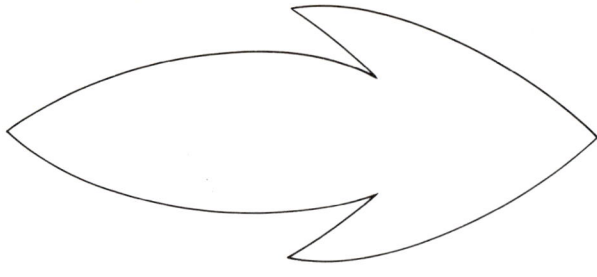

Illustrated opposite

1 (25-cm/10-in) square Rich fruit cake (pages 24–25)
Apricot glaze (page 30)
1.4 kg/3 lb Almond paste (page 31)
1 (30-cm/12-in) square cake board
1.3 kg/2¾ lb Royal icing (page 32)
½ quantity Kneaded fondant icing (page 34)
red and yellow food colourings
1 (2.5-cm/1-in wide) red satin ribbon
1 (1-cm/½-in wide) green satin ribbon

Brush the cake with apricot glaze and cover with almond paste. Allow to dry for a week.

Fix the cake to the board with a dab of royal icing. Reserve about 225 g/8 oz of the icing in an airtight container and use the rest to flat ice the cake. Allow it to dry for 48 hours after applying the second coat.

Meanwhile, colour about two thirds of the fondant bright red and roll it out on a surface lightly dusted with icing sugar. Using a template copied from a real poinsettia leaf or using the one given here, cut 14–16 leaves of various sizes out of the fondant [1]. Mark the leaf veins on each with a sharp knife, curve the leaves slightly and leave them to dry on non-stick paper for 24–48 hours. Or, to make sure they stay curved, drape them over the handle of a wooden spoon [2].

Use the remaining white fondant to mould into five or six Christmas roses (see page 49); allow them to dry.

Place the remaining royal icing in a piping bag fitted with a No. 8 star nozzle and pipe shell borders around the top and bottom edges of the cake. Allow to dry. Build up the poinsettia leaves into a flower in the centre of the cake, securing each leaf to the next with a dab of royal icing [3]. Colour a little icing yellow and pipe small dots in the middle of the poinsettia to resemble stamens. Pipe yellow dots also in the centres of the Christmas roses [4] and arrange these around the poinsettia, fixing them to the cake with icing.

Attach the red ribbon around the sides of the cake and arrange the green one over it.

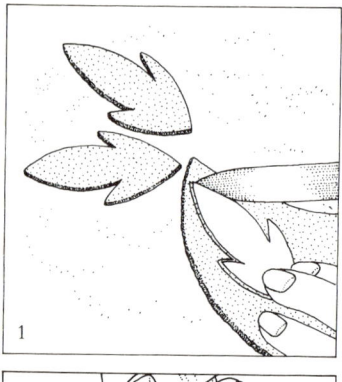
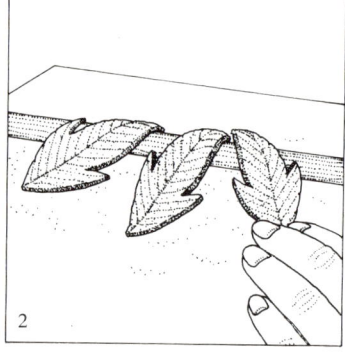
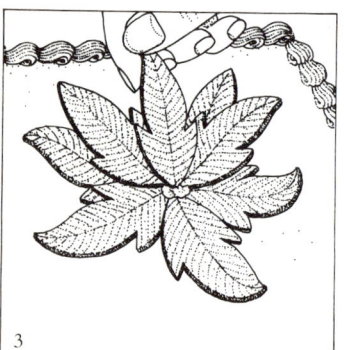
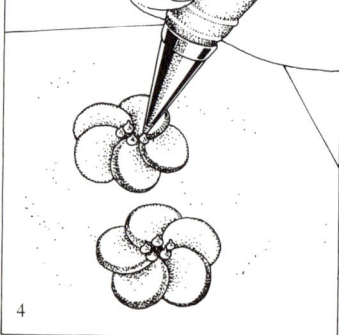

Poinsettia Christmas cake
Robin redbreast Christmas cake (page 88)

FORMAL CAKES

Engagement cake

Illustrated on pages 94–95

1 (20-cm/8-in) square Farmhouse fruit cake (page 26)
Apricot glaze (page 30)
900 g/2 lb Almond paste (page 31)
1½ quantities Kneaded fondant icing (page 34)
1 (25-cm/10-in) square silver cake board
yellow food colouring
350 g/12 oz Royal icing (page 32)
1 (1-cm/½-in wide) white satin ribbon

Brush the cake with apricot glaze and cover it with the almond paste. Allow it to dry out for a week.

Knead the fondant icing until easy to handle. Roll out about 100 g (4 oz) of it on a surface dusted with icing sugar and cut out two heart shapes, about 6 cm (2½ in) high, using either the large heart template given on page 54 or a heart-shaped biscuit cutter. Leave to dry on waxed or non-stick paper for 24 hours.

Use the remaining fondant to cover the cake as for applying almond paste (pages 38–39), but using two long strips for the sides instead of four short ones. Quickly and lightly smooth all the joins and rub the surface of the fondant with hands dusted with icing sugar or cornflour to give it a smooth, shiny texture. Allow it to dry for 24 hours.

Fix the cake to the board with a dab of jam. Add enough yellow food colouring to the royal icing to tint it pale yellow and place it in a piping bag fitted with a No. 2 plain writing nozzle. Pipe a row of large, flat, adjoining dots all along the top edges of the cake [**1**]. Just below each dot, pipe three dots diminishing in size down the sides of the cake, as shown [**2**]. Pipe a scalloped border inside the top edge of the cake to enclose the largest dots [**3**]. Pipe another scalloped line next to this to make a double border. Now pipe a similar row of large, flat, adjoining dots around the bottom edges of the cake where it meets the board and enclose the dots with a single scalloped border on the sides of the cake.

Using the same No. 2 nozzle, write the names of the couple in the fondant hearts, then pipe a border of small dots around the edge of each heart [**4**]. Attach the hearts, slightly overlapping each other, to the top of the cake with a dab of icing. Arrange the ribbon around the side of the cake below the rows of dots and secure it with a pin.

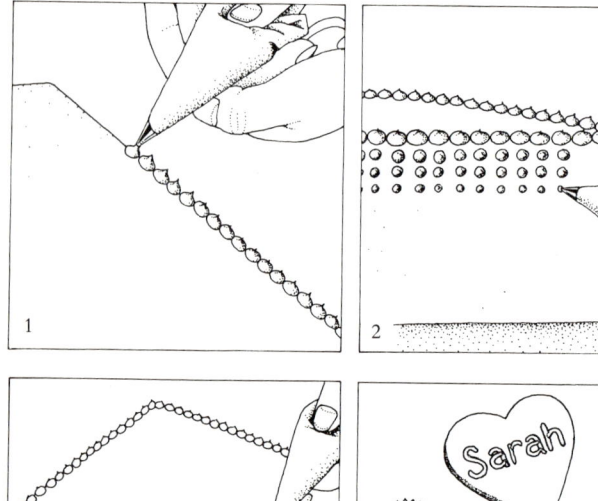

Twenty-first birthday cake

Illustrated on pages 94–95

1 (23-cm/9-in) square Rich fruit cake (pages 24–25)
Apricot glaze (page 30)
1.25 kg/2½ lb Almond paste (page 31)
1.4 kg/3 lb Royal icing (page 32)
food colourings
1 (28-cm/11-in) square cake board

Brush the cake with apricot glaze and cover with almond paste. Leave to dry for a week.

Meanwhile, colour about a quarter of the royal icing a deep yellow ochre. Using the templates given on pages 55 and 56 make run-outs (see page 46) of a key shape and of the number 21 on waxed paper. Leave them to dry for 2–3 days. Keep the remaining ochre icing in a container.

Use the same yellow colouring to give the rest of the white royal icing a pale creamy tint. Fix the cake to the board with a dab of icing. Keep about 4 tablespoons of the cream-coloured icing on one side in an airtight container and flat ice the cake with the rest, taking the icing over the board. Allow it to dry for 48 hours after applying the last coat.

Trace the two triangle designs given on page 53 on to greaseproof paper and cut them out. Position the larger template in one corner on top of the cake and mark round the outline with a pin. Mark the design inside the outline on to the cake too, if liked, for greater accuracy, by pricking through the template. Mark the other three corners in the same way. Use the smaller template to mark the corners round the sides of the cake, bending the template down the middle [1]. Place the reserved yellow ochre icing in a piping bag fitted with a No. 2 plain writing nozzle, and, using the pin marks as a guide, pipe straight lines to form the interlocking triangle design in each corner of the cake top [2]. Pipe the design on the corners round the sides of the cake in the same way [3]. (You may find it helpful to put the cake on a turntable for this.) Finally, use the smaller template again to mark and pipe the design in the middle of each side of the cake.

Change to a No. 3 writing nozzle and pipe a series of large yellow ochre dots around the top and bottom edges of the cake. The dots should be closely spaced but not touching.

Place the reserved cream-coloured icing in a piping bag fitted with a No. 2 nozzle and pipe round the outlines of the run-outs. Allow to dry.

Using the same nozzle, pipe slanted lines over the dots round the top and bottom edges of the cake, as shown [4], curving over the top of one and under the next, for a scroll effect. Fix the key and the 21 run-outs to the cake with dabs of icing.

Overleaf: Rose trellis wedding cake (page 96)
Engagement cake
Twenty-first birthday cake

Rose trellis wedding cake

Illustrated on pages 94–95

1 (15-cm/6-in) square Rich fruit cake (pages 24–25)
1 (23-cm/9-in) square Rich fruit cake (pages 24–25)
1 (30-cm/12-in) square Rich fruit cake (pages 24–25)
Apricot glaze (page 30)
3.4 kg/7½ lb Almond paste (page 31)
1 (20-cm/8-in) square cake board
1 (28-cm/11-in) square cake board
1 (35.5-cm/14-in) square cake board
4.25 kg/9½ lb Royal icing (page 32)
4 (7.5-cm/3-in) cake pillars
4 (5-cm/2-in) cake pillars
yellow food colouring

Brush the three cakes with apricot glaze and cover them with the almond paste. Allow to dry for at least a week.

Secure each cake to its board with royal icing. Use all but 1.25 kg (2½ lb) of the icing to flat ice the cakes and allow to dry for 48 hours after applying the last coat.

Colour 675 g (1½ lb) of the reserved royal icing a pale yellow and place it in a bag fitted with a No. 18 petal nozzle. Pipe about 80 small roses (see page 45), varying slightly in size. You will need 70: the extra 10 will allow for breakages. Leave the roses to dry for at least 24 hours. Reserve the left-over yellow icing in an airtight container.

Using a basket or pyramid mould, pipe a basket of trellis work (see page 44) in white royal icing. Allow it to dry for at least 24 hours.

Trace the large scallop given on page 53 on to greaseproof paper: cut it out to make your template. Mark scallops all along the inside edge of the top of each cake and match this with scallops along the side, as shown [**1**]. Mark two of these pairs of scallops across each top edge of the smallest cake, three across each top edge of the middle tier, and four across each top edge of the largest cake.

Using a No. 1 or 2 plain writing nozzle, fill each pair of scallops with white trellis work (see page 44), piping over the edge of the cake, as shown [**2**]. Outline the scallops in icing to enclose the trellis work. Pipe a line of loops below the scallops along the sides of each cake [**3**]. Pipe a similar line following the scallops on the top of each cake. Pipe three lines radiating outwards down

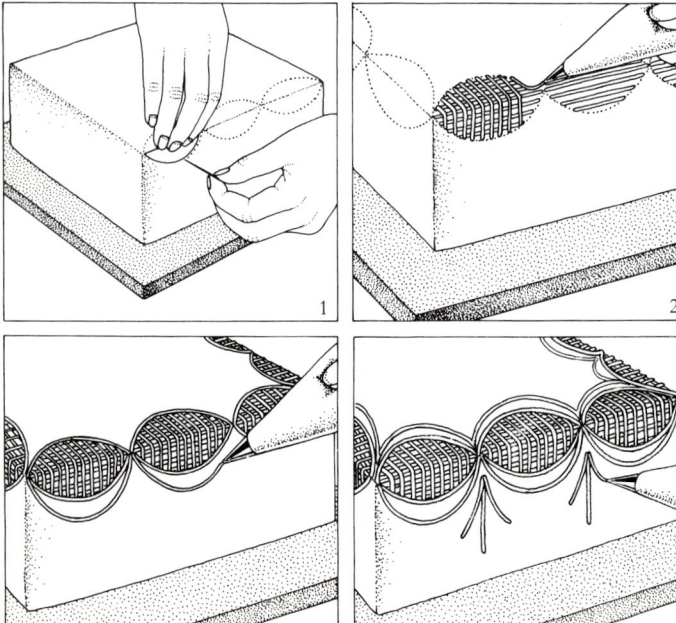
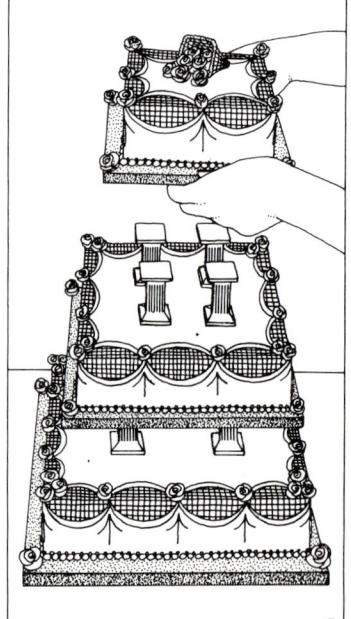

the sides of the cakes between each scallop shape, as shown [4].

Using a No. 2 writing nozzle, pipe a single row of large, white adjoining dots all along the bottom edge of each cake, where the cake meets the board. Allow to dry. Pipe a row of tiny yellow dots just above and between each dot of the first row with a No. 1 or 2 plain writing nozzle.

Arrange the icing roses on the corners and sides of the cake tops, as illustrated (see pages 94–95), using 24 for the largest cake, 16 for the next and 8 for the last. Fix them in place with a little royal icing. Fix four more roses on each cake board at the corners of the cakes.

Gently ease the trellis basket from its mould and arrange it on the smallest cake. Fill it with the ten remaining roses, securing with a little royal icing.

Assemble the cake [5], using the taller pillars on the lowest tier. Secure the pillars with dabs of icing at the base.

Ivory wedding cake

Illustrated on page 99

1 (15-cm/6-in) round Rich fruit cake (pages 24–25)
1 (20-cm/8-in) round Rich fruit cake (pages 24–25)
1 (25-cm/10-in) round Rich fruit cake (pages 24–25)
1 (30-cm/12-in) round Rich fruit cake (pages 24–25)
Apricot glaze (page 30)
3.75 kg/8½ lb Almond paste (page 31)
6–7 quantities Kneaded fondant icing (page 34)
yellow food colouring
1 (15-cm/6-in) cake card
1 (20-cm/8-in) cake card
1 (25-cm/10-in) cake card
1 (35.5-cm/14-in) cake board
225 g/8 oz Royal icing (page 32)
pieces of asparagus fern

Brush the cakes with apricot glaze and cover with almond paste. Allow to dry for a week.

Knead the fondant until it is easy to handle and work in a very little yellow food colouring to tint it pale ivory. Use about 350 g (12 oz) of the fondant to cover the first cake; 450 g (1 lb) for the second; 575 g (1¼ lb) for the third and 800 g (1¾ lb) for the fourth. Roll each portion out to a round 7.5 cm (3 in) larger in diameter than the cake to be iced. Mould the rounds on to the cakes to cover them completely (see page 86) and allow to dry for 24 hours.

Use the remaining fondant icing to mould 70–90 ivory-coloured roses as for almond paste flowers (see page 48), varying in size from tiny rose-buds to full-blown roses. Leave them to dry on waxed paper for 24 hours.

Fix the largest cake on the cake board and the smaller cakes on their corresponding cake cards with a little royal icing. Stack the cakes on top of each other, taking care to centre them.

Tint the royal icing ivory and place it in a piping bag fitted with a No. 4 trefoil nozzle. Pipe a trefoil border around the bottom edge of each cake [1].

Arrange the fondant roses in a spiral down the cake tiers, fixing them with icing [2]. Decorate with sprigs of fern.

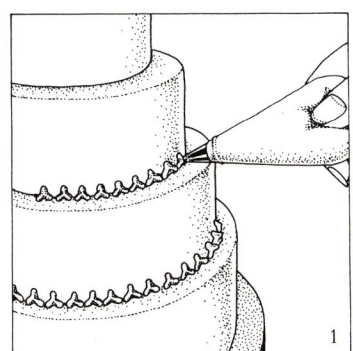
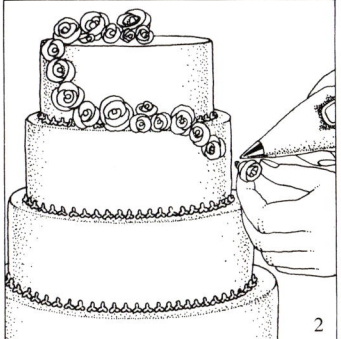

American wedding cake

1 quantity Basic Victoria sandwich mixture (page 21)
3 quantities Basic Victoria sandwich mixture (page 21)
5 quantities Basic Victoria sandwich mixture (page 21), made with an extra 100 g/4 oz flour
1 (35.5-cm/14-in) round cake board
1 (15-cm/6-in) round cake card
1 (23-cm/9-in) round cake card
7 quantities Brandy butter cream (page 28)
3 round silver cake pillars
10 red fondant roses (as for almond paste flowers, page 48)
bought green artificial leaves
pieces of asparagus fern

Set the oven at moderate (160 C, 325 F, gas 3). Grease and base-line one 15-cm (6-in) round cake tin, one 23-cm (9-in) round tin and one 30-cm (12-in) round tin and fill each with its appropriate cake mixture. Bake the cakes for 55 minutes, $1\frac{1}{4}$ hours and 1 hour 40 minutes respectively until each is firm and golden and beginning to shrink away from the side of the tin. Turn the cakes out on to a wire rack and leave them to cool.

Position the largest cake in the centre of the cake board and the two smaller ones on their respective cake cards, securing each with a dab of butter cream.

Spread an even layer of butter cream over each cake, smoothing the top and side with a palette knife or an icing ruler. Use 1 quantity of the butter cream to cover the smallest cake, about $1\frac{1}{2}$ quantities for the middle tier and 2 quantities for the largest cake. Keep the rest of the icing on one side for piping.

Assemble the cakes into three tiers, placing the pillars on the middle tier to support the top one. Using a No. 12 shell nozzle, pipe the remaining butter cream in shell borders around the top and bottom edges of the cakes. Pile a few red fondant roses on the top cake together with the green leaves. Arrange the rest of the roses and the pieces of fern on the lower tiers and on the cake board.

Ivory wedding cake (page 97)

Butterfly wedding cake

Illustrated on page 103

1 (30-cm/12-in) square Rich fruit cake (pages 24–25)
2 kg/4½ lb Almond paste (page 31)
Apricot glaze (page 30)
2 kg/4½ lb Royal icing (page 32)
1 (40.5-cm/16-in) square cake board
silver sugar balls
silver horseshoe or heart decorations

Using a very sharp knife, carefully slice the cake horizontally in half. Dust a work surface lightly with icing sugar and roll out about 350 g (12 oz) of the almond paste to a 30-cm (12-in) square. Brush the paste with apricot glaze and place one half of the cake on to it, cut side down.

Turn the cake half over, brush the other side of almond paste with more apricot glaze and place the second half of the cake on top so that the almond paste is sandwiched between the two. Brush the top and sides of the cake with apricot glaze and use the remaining almond paste to cover it in the usual way. Allow the paste to dry out for a week.

Trace the small butterfly wing design given here on to a piece of card, place a sheet of waxed or non-stick paper over it and make eight run-outs (see page 46) in white royal icing, plus a few extras in case of breakages [**1**]. Now trace the design again on to another piece of card but this time reverse it; make eight more run-outs, plus extras, so that you end up with eight pairs of butterfly wings.

Make four or more run-outs of the large corner wings using the template given here. Allow all the run-outs to dry for 2–3 days.

Fix the cake to the board with a dab of royal icing. Use 1.6 kg (3½ lb) of the royal icing to flat ice the cake, taking the icing to the edge of the board, if liked. Allow the cake to dry for at least 48 hours after applying the last coat.

Using the larger template, mark the corner wing design on the top of the cake: position the template in the middle of each side, about 1 cm (½ in) in from the edge, and mark round the outline with a pin [**2**]. The outlines should all join up to form a square on the diagonal in the centre of the cake.

Using a No. 2 plain writing nozzle, pipe a continuous line of royal icing around the outer edge of the curved design. Allow this to dry, then pipe another line directly on top of the first [**3**].

Change to a No. 12 shell

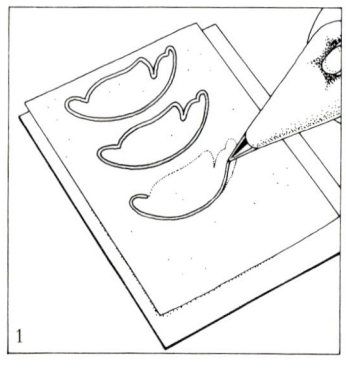
1

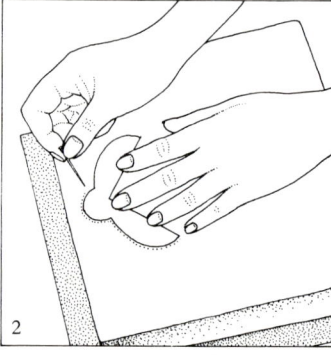
2

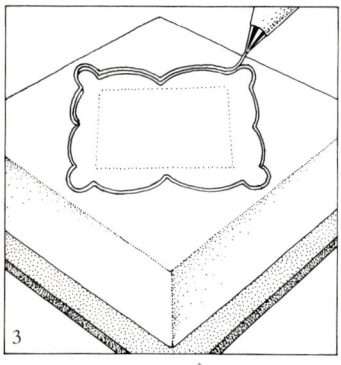
3

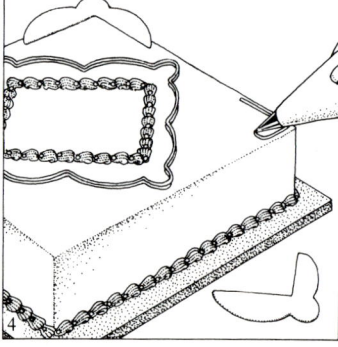
4

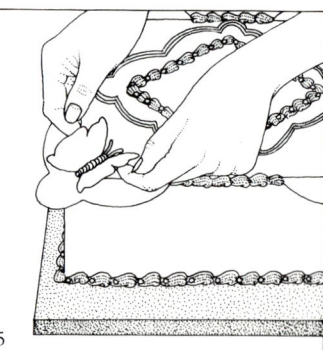
5

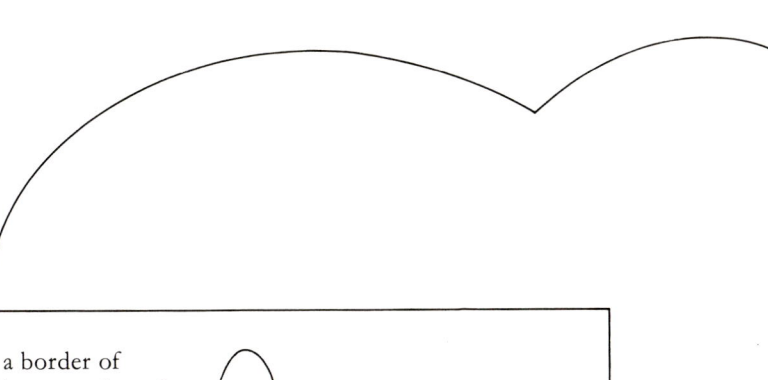

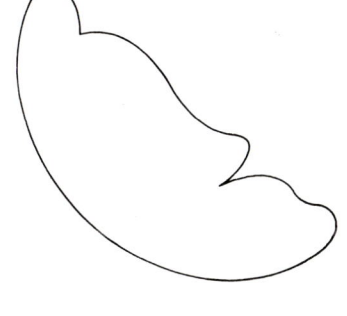

nozzle and pipe a border of shells along the bottom edge of the cake where the cake meets the board. Place a small silver ball between each shell.

Pipe a shell border around the centre square on top of the cake following your pin marks and decorate it with the silver balls in the same way.

Carefully ease the dried run-outs from the waxed or non-stick paper. Pipe a fine line of royal icing on each top corner of the cake [4] and use it to attach the corner wings. Support the wings while the icing is drying by propping kitchen paper or foil underneath them. Pipe shell borders along the top edges of the cake between the wings.

Using a No. 3 plain writing nozzle held close to the surface of the cake, pipe a continuous spiral of icing straight on to the cake at each corner to make the butterfly bodies. Pipe tiny antennae at the ends of the bodies. Secure one pair of wings on each body at an angle of about 45° to the cake, as shown [5]. Support these too while they dry by placing small pieces of kitchen paper underneath them. Make up four more butterflies in the same way, one in the centre of each side of the cake.

Finally attach the silver horseshoe or hearts to the centre of the cake, using icing piped from a shell nozzle to prop them up. Decorate with a few silver balls.

Lace-edged wedding cake

Illustrated opposite

1 (18-cm/7-in) round Rich fruit cake (pages 24–25)
1 (28-cm/11-in) round Rich fruit cake (pages 24–25)
Apricot glaze (page 30)
1.8 kg/4 lb Almond paste (page 31)
1 (20-cm/8-in) round cake board
1 (35.5-cm/14-in) round cake board
2.1 kg/4¾ lb Royal icing (page 32)
1 (1.7-m/5 ft 6-in long) white satin ribbon, 2.5 cm/1 in wide
4 hexagonal white cake pillars
small silver-coloured vase
lily-of-the-valley or freesias

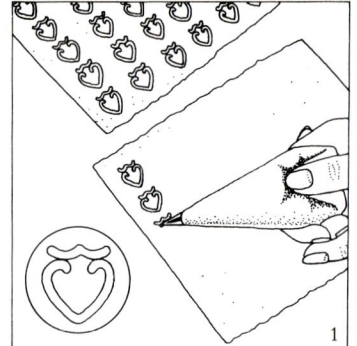
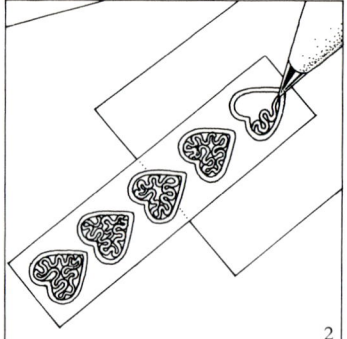
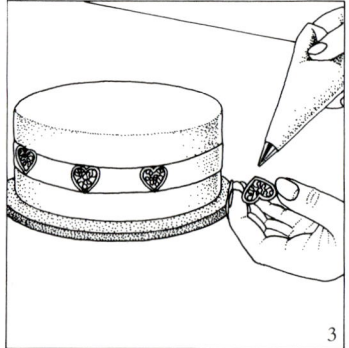
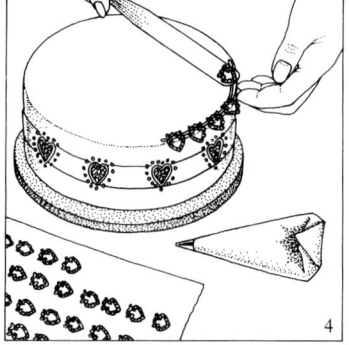

Brush each cake with apricot glaze and cover it with almond paste. Allow the paste to dry for at least a week. Fix the cakes to the boards with royal icing, then flat ice them with all but 450 g/1 lb of the icing. Leave to dry for 48 hours after applying the last coat.

Place the remaining icing in a piping bag fitted with a No. 1 or 2 plain writing nozzle. Pipe lace pieces directly on to waxed paper, beginning with a tiny, curly, double scalloped shape. Beneath this pipe a heart shape [**1**]. Make about 200 of these lace pieces to allow a margin for breakages and leave them to dry. Then go over each piece again, piping tiny dots at intervals on the outline of the heart shape.

Trace the smallest heart template given on page 54 on to a piece of card, cover with waxed or non-stick paper and pipe about 20 lacy hearts. Begin by piping the outline, then fill in the centre with lace work [**2**]. Leave to dry.

Arrange the satin ribbon around the cakes and secure at the join with a dab of royal icing. Carefully peel the waxed or non-stick paper off the lace hearts. Pipe a little icing on the backs of the hearts and fix them at intervals around the ribbon [**3**]. Surround each heart with a border of tiny dots.

To attach the lace, pipe a fine line of royal icing round the top edge of each cake. Pipe a little of the line at a time to prevent it drying out. Lifting the lace pieces from the waxed paper with a palette knife, fix them along the line, pointing out from the cake [**4**]. Do the same along the bottom edges, fixing the lace to the cake boards.

Pipe a single border of very fine dots along the lace on the top and round the bottom of each cake. Pipe another more widely spaced border next to the first.

Position the pillars on the larger cake and mark round them with a pin. Remove the pillars and pipe a double row of tiny dots around the pin marks. Do the same with the silver vase on the smaller cake.

Assemble the cakes just before serving, fixing the pillars in place with a little royal icing. Arrange the flowers in the vase.

Lace-edged wedding cake
Butterfly wedding cake (page 100)

Daisy christening cake

Illustrated on page 107

1 (20-cm/8-in) round Rich fruit cake (pages 24–25)
Apricot glaze (page 30)
675 g/1½ lb Almond paste (page 31)
1 lb/450 g Royal icing (page 32)
silver sugar balls
1 quantity Kneaded fondant icing (page 34)
pink food colouring
1 (25-cm/10-in) round silver cake board

Brush the cake with apricot glaze and cover it with the almond paste. Allow the paste to dry for at least a week. On waxed or non-stick paper, make an oval run-out (see page 46) large enough for the name to be piped on, using white royal icing and the large oval template given on page 53, if liked. Allow it to dry out for 2–3 days.

Place some royal icing in a piping bag fitted with a No. 18 petal nozzle and pipe 30–35 small daises (see page 45) on to waxed or non-stick paper. Decorate the centre of each daisy with a silver ball. Allow them to dry.

Knead the fondant until easy to handle and work in enough pink food colouring to colour it pale pink. Roll it out on a surface lightly dusted with icing sugar or cornflour to a 28-cm/11-in round and use it to cover the cake, easing it gently down the side (see page 86). Trim round the base of the cake with a sharp knife and fix the cake to the board with a dab of royal icing. Allow the cake to dry for 24 hours before decorating it.

Using white royal icing and a No. 8 trefoil nozzle, pipe a series of stars, about 1 cm (½ in) apart, around the top edge of the cake [**1**].

Mark the icing on the side of the cake with a pin at 1-cm (½-in) intervals, 1 cm (½ in) above the cake board. Using a No. 2 plain writing nozzle, pipe a border of scallops around the cake, following the pin marks, as shown [**2**]. Mark the same design on the cake board, about 5 mm (¼ in) from the cake, and pipe the scalloped border as before [**3**]. Allow to dry. Using a No. 1 or 2 plain

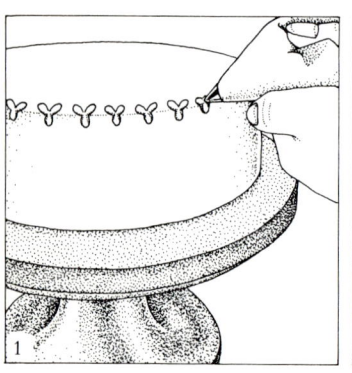

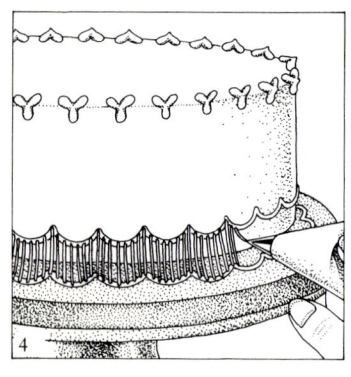
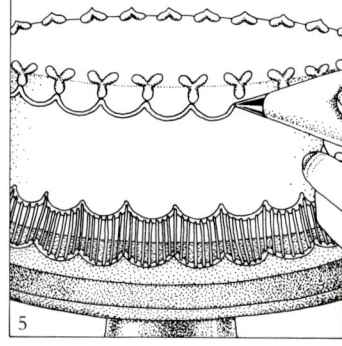
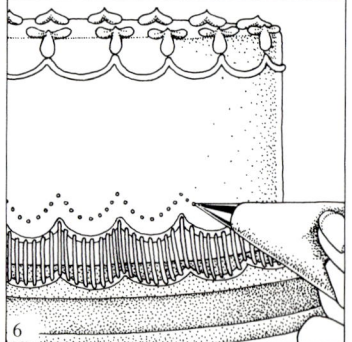

writing nozzle, pipe hanging lines of icing from the scallops on the cake to meet those on the board [4]. Now pipe a scalloped border just below the top edge of the cake, linking the trefoil stars, as shown [5]. Using a No. 1 nozzle, follow the shape of the scalloped border round the bottom edge of the cake with tiny, even-sized dots [6].

Colour a little royal icing pale pink, place it in a bag fitted with a No. 2 plain writing nozzle and pipe the name on the oval run-out. Allow it to dry. Carefully peel the waxed or non-stick paper from the run-out and position it on the cake, fixing it in place with a dab of icing. Use icing again to attach the daisies in groups on the top and side of the cake.

Iced fancies

Illustrated on page 107

1 quantity Genoese sponge mixture (page 22)
Apricot glaze (page 30)
175 g/6 oz Almond paste (page 31)
pink, yellow and blue food colourings
1 quantity Boiled fondant icing (page 33)
crystallised rose petals and violets, mimosa balls

Set the oven at moderate (180 C, 350 F, gas 4). Grease and line a 23-cm (9-in) square cake tin. Turn the cake mixture into this and bake it for 30–35 minutes or until golden and firm. Turn out and cool on a wire rack.

When cool, cut the cake into rectangles, triangles, rounds, diamonds and heart shapes, as shown [1], using biscuit cutters and a sharp knife. Brush the pieces of cake with apricot glaze and arrange them on a wire rack with a baking tray underneath to catch the fondant.

Colour the almond paste with different food colourings and model it into tiny balls, rolls and cubes; place these on top of the cakes [2].

Keep about a quarter of the fondant on one side for piping and divide the rest into four parts. Place each part in a small bowl and warm it separately with a little stock syrup over a pan of hot water to a pouring consistency (27–30 C/80–85 F). Colour one portion pale pink, one yellow, one blue and leave one white. Pour each colour of fondant over some of the cakes to coat them as smoothly as possible and leave the cakes to dry for about 1 hour.

Warm the reserved fondant until it reaches a piping consistency (see page 34). Colour half of it pink. Using a No. 2 plain writing nozzle and a No. 12 shell nozzle, pipe pink and white lines, zig-zags or petal patterns on the cakes [3]. Decorate with the crystallised roses, violets and mimosa balls.

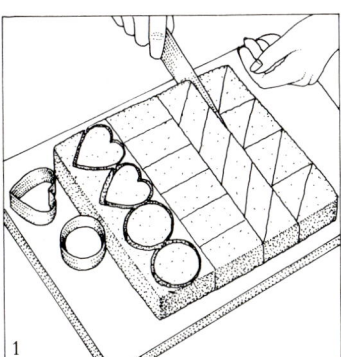
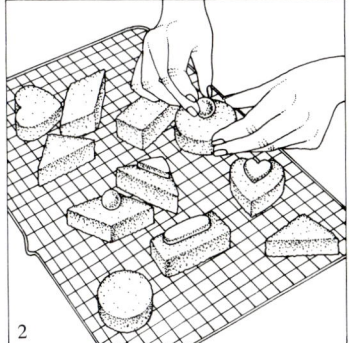
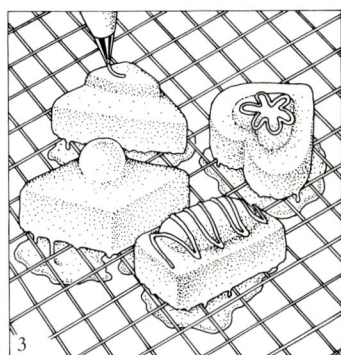

Crib christening cake

Illustrated opposite

1 (23-cm/9-in) square Rich fruit cake (pages 24–25)
Apricot glaze (page 30)
1.25 kg/2½ lb Almond paste (page 31)
1.4 kg/3 lb Royal icing (page 32)
¼ quantity Kneaded fondant icing (page 34)
blue food colouring
1 (35.5-cm/14-in) cake board

Brush the cake with apricot glaze and cover it with almond paste. Allow it to dry for a week.

Make run-out letters (see page 46) for the name in white royal icing on waxed paper, using the designs given on the endpapers, if liked. Leave to dry for 2–3 days.

Colour half the fondant icing pale blue and mould it into a small oval crib with a hood and two rockers. Use the remaining white fondant to mould a baby's head, pillow and blanket, as shown [1], marking a criss-cross pattern on the blanket with a knife. Assemble the crib and allow it to dry for 24 hours.

Fix the cake diagonally on the cake board with a little royal icing. Colour about 1 kg (2¼ lb) of the icing pale blue and use it to flat ice the cake, using a serrated icing comb when applying the final coat to the sides to give a ribbed effect.

Allow to dry for 48 hours.

Make a template of a 13-cm (5-in) square, position it diagonally on the cake and mark round it with a pin. Colour about a third of the remaining white royal icing pale blue. Using a No. 2 plain writing nozzle, pipe a series of straight lines in groups of two across the square, parallel with two sides of the square [2]. Turn the cake and pipe a second layer of lines in the opposite direction. Allow to dry.

Pipe round the outline of the square [3] in white icing, using a No. 2 nozzle. Allow to dry, then pipe a second outline over the first. Pipe three groups of two parallel lines in each corner of the cake board [4].

Change to a No. 8 star nozzle and pipe a star border around the top and bottom edges of the cake and down each corner. Allow to dry. Pipe a tiny blue dot in the centre of each star [5] and at the end of each of the lines on the board.

Carefully remove the run-out letters from the paper and arrange them on the lattice square, with the fondant crib.

Crib christening cake
Daisy christening cake (page 104)
Iced fancies (page 105)

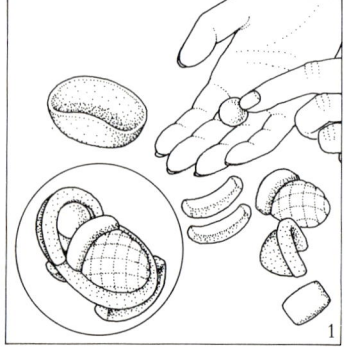

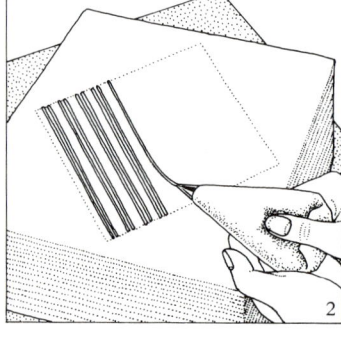

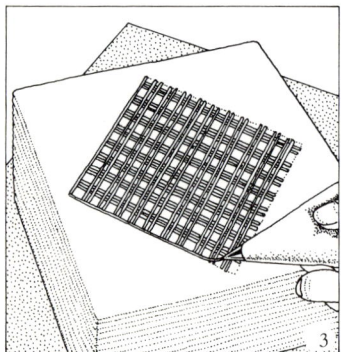

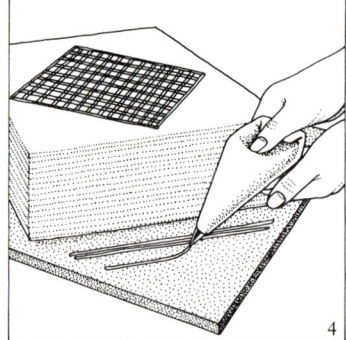

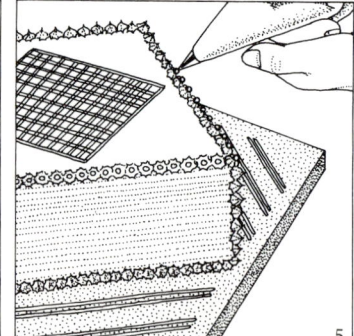

Silver Wedding cake

Illustrated on pages 6–7

1 (25-cm/10-in) square Rich fruit cake (pages 24–25)
Apricot glaze (page 30)
1.4 kg/3 lb Almond paste (page 31)
1 (30-cm/12-in) square silver cake board
1.4 kg/3 lb Royal icing (page 32)
silver food colouring
silver sugar balls
1 (2.5-cm/1-in wide) silver cake ribbon
a few purchased silver leaves

Brush the cake with apricot glaze and cover it with the almond paste. Leave it to dry for at least a week.

Fix the cake to the board with a dab of royal icing. Use 1.25 kg (2½ lb) of the icing to flat ice the cake and allow it to dry for 48 hours after applying the last coat. Using the templates given on page 56, make royal icing run-outs (see page 46) to make the number 25 on waxed or non-stick paper; allow them to dry for 48 hours. Pipe tiny dots of icing around the edges of the run-outs with a No. 1 fine writing nozzle. Allow these to dry, then paint silver food colouring on the dots with a fine brush.

Place all the remaining icing in a piping bag fitted with a No. 12 shell nozzle and pipe shells along the top edges of the cake, alternately curving inwards and outwards, as shown [**1**]. Place a silver ball between each shell.

Change to a No. 2 plain writing nozzle and pipe a single fine line of icing all round the top of the cake, about 1 cm (½ in) inside the top edge [**2**]. Pipe three right-angled lines in each corner of the cake top, one inside the other, as shown [**3**]. Arrange a silver ball at either end of the longest corner lines. Pipe the same design in the middle of each side of the cake, with the right-angle pointing upwards to form an arrow shape [**4**] and the lines extending to exactly 2.5 cm (1 in) above the cake board. Allow to dry, then fit the silver ribbon around the bottom of the cake and secure it at the join with a little icing.

Carefully remove the run-out numbers from the waxed or non-stick paper and arrange them with the silver leaves in the centre of the cake. Fix them in place with a little royal icing.

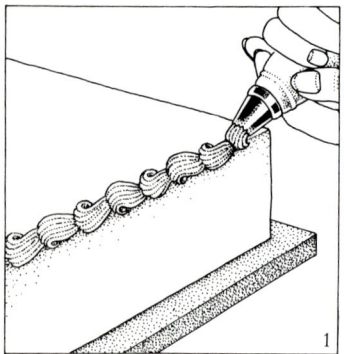
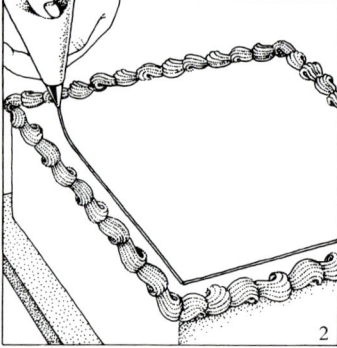
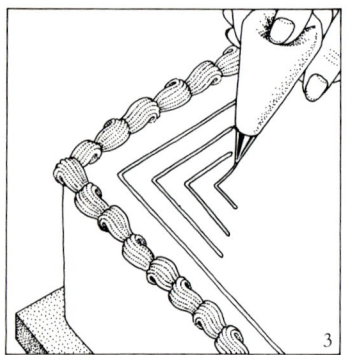
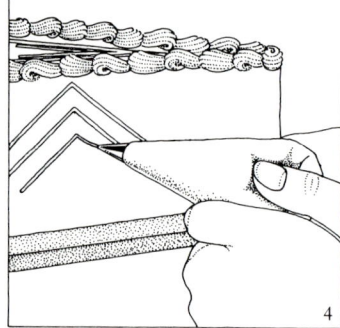

Golden Wedding cake

Illustrated on page 111

Rich fruit cake mixture for a 20-cm/8-in round tin (pages 24–25)
Apricot glaze (page 30)
1.25 kg/2½ lb Almond paste (page 31)
1 (25-cm/10-in) square gold cake board
1.4 kg/3 lb Royal icing (page 32)
a little granulated sugar
gold ribbon
12 purchased plastic gold bells

Set the oven at cool (150 C, 300 F, gas 2). Grease and line a 1.75-litre (3-pint) hexagonal cake tin, measuring 23 cm (9 in) across to opposite corners. Put the cake mixture in the tin and bake it for 2¼–2½ hours until firm and a skewer inserted in the centre comes out clean. Turn out and cool on a wire rack.

Brush the cake with apricot glaze and cover it with the almond paste. Allow the paste to dry for at least a week.

Fix the cake to the board with a dab of royal icing. Use about three quarters of the icing to flat ice the cake and allow it to dry for 48 hours after applying the last coat. In white royal icing and using the templates given on page 56, make run-outs (see page 46) for the number 50 on to waxed or non-stick paper. Leave them for several hours until almost dry, then sprinkle lightly with granulated sugar so that just a little sticks on the surface for sparkle. Allow to dry completely for 24–48 hours.

Place the remaining royal icing in a piping bag fitted with a No. 12 shell nozzle. Pipe a border of shells around the top edge of the cake with the 'tails' of the shells pointing out from the cake, as shown [1]. Pipe a similar border around the bottom edge so that the shells spread out on to the board [2]. Allow the icing to dry.

Attach a band of gold ribbon around the sides of the cake with a little icing. Cut the rest of the ribbon into 10–12 short, thin strips and shape them into curls with a pair of scissors. Hold one end of each ribbon in one hand and, holding the scissors in the other, pull the blade firmly down the length of the ribbon to curl it, as shown [3].

Fix the number 50 on top of the cake with a little royal icing and surround it with a few swirls of curled ribbon. Tie the gold bells into pairs with more pieces of curled ribbon and arrange them in the corners of the cake.

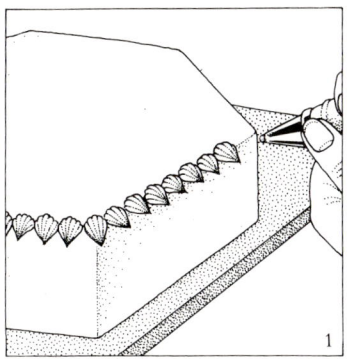
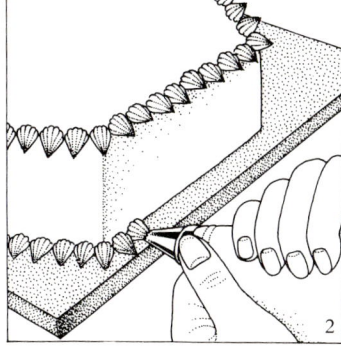
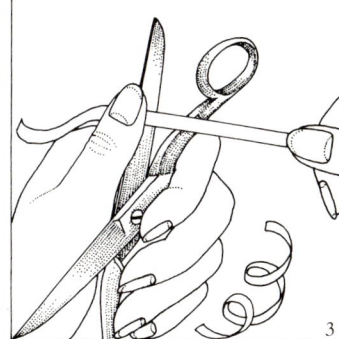

Almond and fondant petits fours

Illustrated opposite

450 g/1 lb Almond paste (page 31)
450 g/1 lb Kneaded fondant icing (page 34)
food colourings
peppermint essence
vanilla essence
a few drops of brandy
225 g/8 oz dessert chocolate
Apricot glaze (page 30)
desiccated coconut, toasted
crystallised rose petals and violets
mimosa balls
flaked almonds
walnut halves

Knead the almond paste and fondant separately on a surface lightly dusted with icing sugar until they are easy to handle.

Divide the almond paste into three; leave one part yellow and colour the other two green and pink respectively. Roll out an equal portion of each colour to a thin rectangle and stack the pieces one on top of another; cut the paste into slices to show the layers [**1**].

Roll out another portion of each colour of paste to a wider rectangle and pile these pieces one on top of the other. Roll up the paste from the longest side of the rectangle, like a Swiss roll [**2**]. Cut this into slices to show the spiral design.

Roll out any remaining almond paste and stamp out decorative shapes with small cocktail biscuit cutters.

Divide the fondant into two portions. Colour one portion green and knead in a few drops of peppermint essence. Flavour half the other portion with vanilla essence and half with brandy. Roll out all three kinds of fondant and stamp it into shapes with the biscuit cutters.

Melt the chocolate gently in a bowl over a pan of hot water. Dip some of the petits fours into it until partly covered and some to cover completely. Brush other shapes with apricot glaze and toss them in toasted coconut [**3**].

Decorate the petits fours with crystallised flowers, mimosa balls and pieces of almond or walnut.

Golden Wedding cake (page 109)
Almond and fondant petits fours

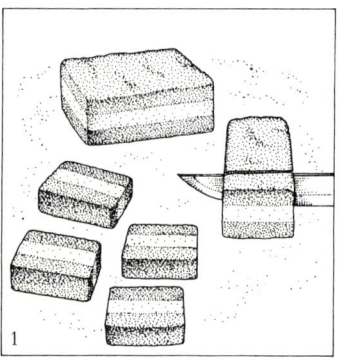
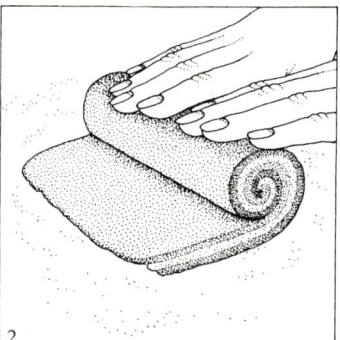
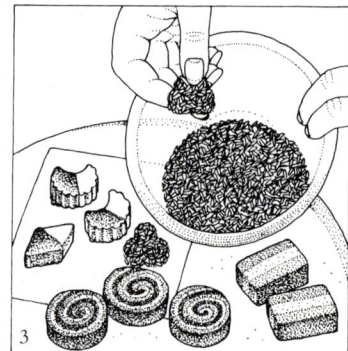

CHILDREN'S PARTY CAKES

While many children's tastes seem to run to the savoury rather than the sweet, a well-iced cake is still the crowning highlight of a party tea. Few will resist the temptation of sampling luscious chocolate icing or breaking up an original design shaped, say, in the form of a railway engine – off with the funnel and who'll eat the wheels?

Thinking up new ideas is only one part of the problem – carrying them out is the main headache for a mother in a hurry, but with a few basic techniques at her fingertips, producing a cake to appeal to the younger members of the family is no more difficult than, for instance, preparing a festive cake for Christmas. Just a little imagination, and a clue to the favourite colours and flavours, and you're away.

Children love biscuits, too; animal shapes and biscuits with funny faces will always be winners, and you can ring the changes with shapes and patterns according to your fancy. Chocolate buttons and smarties are great standbys as ready-made eyes and ears, and you can try a different approach by piping chocolate lettering on plain-topped biscuits – imagine, an alphabet to choose from so they can spell out their names!

There's a lot of pleasure to be gained in thinking up new ideas to appeal to children and devising something appropriate to the special occasion. Mind you, the only reward you're likely to get beyond the initial gasp of surprise is the looks of concentration as your wonderful, original, carefully iced creations are demolished and reduced to crumbs.

Parcel cake

Illustrated on page 115

2½ quantities Basic Victoria sandwich mixture (page 21)
8 tablespoons black cherry or blackcurrant jam
Apricot glaze (page 30)
double quantity Kneaded fondant icing (page 34)
food colourings
1 (25-cm/10-in) square cake board
225 g/8 oz Royal icing (page 32)

Set the oven at moderate (180 C, 350 F, gas 4). Grease and line a 20-cm (8-in) square cake tin and turn the mixture into it. Bake it for about 1 hour 10 minutes or until firm and golden. Turn out and leave the cake to cool on a wire rack.

Split the cake horizontally into three even layers and sandwich them back together with the jam.

Brush the top and sides of the cake with apricot glaze. Keep about one third of the fondant on one side and knead a little pink food colouring into the rest. Roll this out on a surface dusted with icing sugar and use it to cover the cake in the same way as applying almond paste (see pages 38–39), but using two long strips for the sides instead of four short ones. Trim any surplus fondant from the base of the cake and fix the cake to the board with a dab of jam.

Reserve about 50 g (2 oz) of the remaining fondant and colour the rest pale blue. Roll out two long strips about 2.5 cm (1 in) wide and fit them over the cake, crossing them

near the centre like a ribbon [**1**]. Mould four short separate strips to form a bow: fold over two of the pieces into loops to make the bow shape and arrange them on the cake where the ribbons cross; trim one end of each of the two remaining pieces with a knife to give them a ribbon finish and fasten these to the bow [**2**]. Cover the join with a short piece of fondant, as shown [**3**]. Allow the cake to dry for 24 hours.

Roll out the reserved piece of white fondant and cut it into a gift tag shape, using the template given here. Leave this to dry on waxed or non-stick paper for 24 hours.

Colour all but 2 tablespoons of the royal icing a clear forget-me-not blue and place it in a bag fitted with a No. 2 plain writing nozzle. Pipe a 'Best Wishes' message on the tag [**4**], then arrange the tag on the cake and fix it in place with a little icing.

Decorate the parcel with tiny forget-me-nots: pipe rings of blue dots at intervals all over the cake with the No. 2 nozzle [**5**]; place the reserved white icing in a piping bag also fitted with a No. 2 nozzle and pipe a dot in the centre of each flower. Allow the icing to dry.

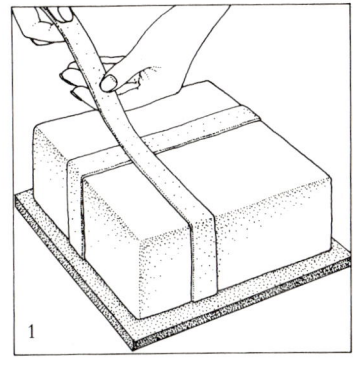
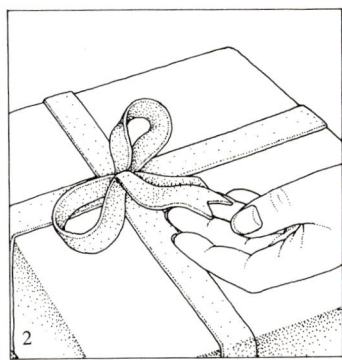
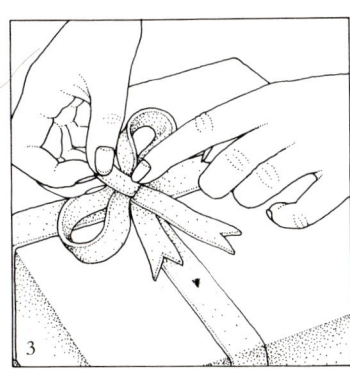
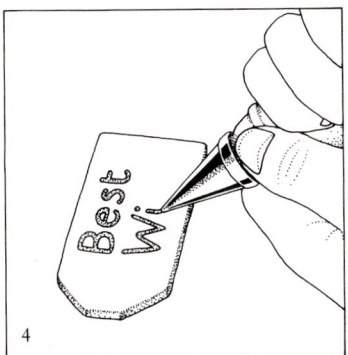

CHILDREN'S PARTY CAKES

Drum cake

4 Basic one-stage or Victoria sandwich cakes (page 21)
8–9 tablespoons jam
1 (20-cm/8-in) round cake board
1½ quantities Butter cream (page 28)
225 g/8 oz Almond paste (page 31)
food colourings
2 drinking straws

Sandwich all four cakes together with the jam and place the cake on the board. Use about two thirds of the butter cream to cover the cake, smoothing with an icing ruler or a palette knife.

Colour about three quarters of the almond paste bright red. Roll it out into two wide, flat strips, each long enough to fit round the side of the cake. Arrange one around the top edge and the other around the base [1], pressing the ends together to join.

Colour the reserved butter icing bright blue. Using a No. 3 plain writing nozzle, pipe blue criss-cross lines around the side of the drum, running between the two strips of paste [2]. Pipe a birthday message on the cake top.

Colour the remaining almond paste bright yellow. Mould it into two balls and fit these on the straws to make drumsticks.

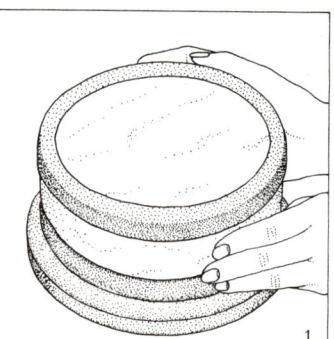
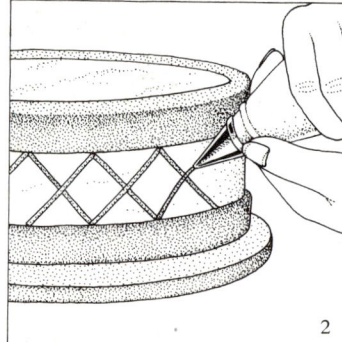

Parcel cake (page 112)
Iced peanut biscuits (page 117)
Chocolate train cake (page 116)

Chocolate train cake

Illustrated on page 115

1 quantity Chocolate-flavoured Victoria sandwich mixture (page 21)
1 Chocolate-flavoured Swiss roll (page 23), rolled in greaseproof paper and cooled
1 quantity Vanilla butter cream (page 28)
2 (150-g/5.3-oz) packets plain chocolate cake covering
1 (30-cm/12-in) square cake board (optional)
small coloured sweets
piece of cotton wool
cocktail stick

Set the oven at moderate (180 C, 350 F, gas 4). Grease and base-line a 15-cm (6-in) square cake tin. Spoon the cake mixture into it and bake for 40–45 minutes until firm and beginning to shrink away from the sides of the tin. Turn the cake out to cool on a wire rack.

Unroll the Swiss roll, spread it with about half the butter cream and roll it up again. Cut four 1-cm (½-in) thick slices from one end and keep them on one side.

Slice the square sandwich cake into two equal rectangles and cut a 3.5-cm/1½-in wide piece off the end of each. Arrange the uncut portion of Swiss roll first on a wire cake rack to make the engine; leave a gap, then stand one rectangle upright behind it for the cabin with the other lying horizontally behind the first to make the truck. Position one of the 3.5-cm/1½-in pieces on top of the horizontal rectangle, near the upright one, as shown [**1**]. Trim down the remaining piece of cake to make a funnel and keep this on one side.

Melt the chocolate cake covering gently in a bowl held over a pan of hot water. Pour it over the two main parts of the train, coating each separately, as shown [**2**]. Fix the funnel in the chocolate near the front of the train and coat this too [**3**]. Allow the chocolate to dry.

Assemble the train on a long plate or a cake board. Arrange the four slices of Swiss roll against the sides to form wheels. Place the remaining butter cream in a piping bag fitted with a No. 8 star nozzle and pipe star borders all around the edges of the train [**4**]. Change to a No. 3 plain writing nozzle and pipe windows on the side of the cabin and a face on the front of the engine, using two sweets for eyes. Pile the rest of the sweets in the truck.

Fit the cotton wool over the cocktail stick to make the steam and insert it in the funnel.

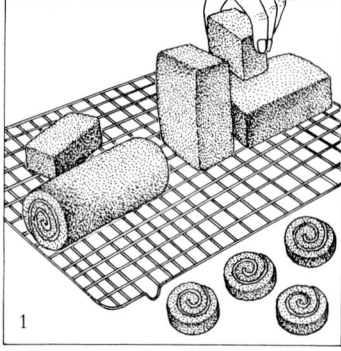
1

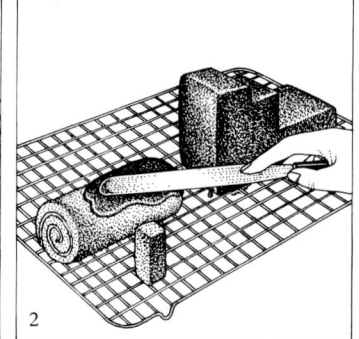
2

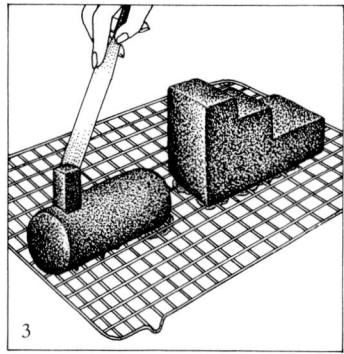
3

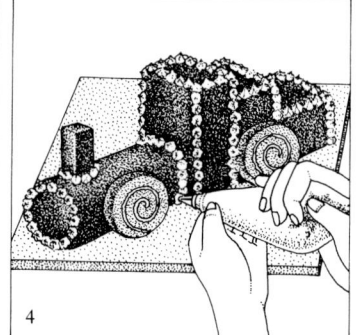
4

Iced peanut biscuits

Illustrated on page 115

75 g/3 oz butter or margarine
225 g/8 oz peanut butter
175 g/6 oz soft light brown sugar
1 egg
½ teaspoon vanilla essence
175 g/6 oz plain flour
1 teaspoon baking powder
¼ teaspoon salt
1 quantity Glacé icing (page 29)
75 g/3 oz dessert chocolate
a few unsalted peanuts

Set the oven at moderately hot (190 C, 375 F, gas 5). Cream the butter or margarine with the peanut butter until smooth. Add the sugar, and cream again until light and fluffy. Beat in the egg and vanilla essence. Sift together the flour, baking powder and salt and fold the dry ingredients into the butter mixture, mixing thoroughly. Chill for about 30 minutes.

Roll the dough out on a lightly floured surface and stamp it into about 30 (6-cm/2½-in) rounds with a biscuit cutter. Place the rounds at intervals on greased baking sheets, allowing space for the biscuits to spread. Bake them for about 10 minutes or until firm and golden. Transfer the biscuits to a wire rack to cool.

Flood the tops of the biscuits with glacé icing and allow them to dry. Melt the chocolate gently in a bowl over a pan of hot water and place it in a greaseproof piping bag. Snip off the tip of the bag and drizzle chocolate over the biscuits, piping names, initials and patterns, as liked. Allow the chocolate to dry and decorate some of the biscuits with a few chopped peanuts.

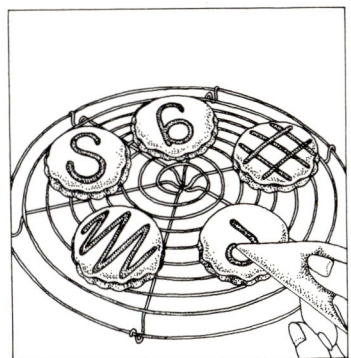

Funny face lollipop biscuits

Illustrated on the front cover

50 g/2 oz butter or margarine
25 g/1 oz caster sugar
1 egg, beaten
100 g/4 oz plain flour
8 flat wooden lollipop sticks
1 quantity Glacé icing (page 29)
food colourings
small coloured sweets

Set the oven at moderate (160 C, 325 F, gas 3). Cream together the fat and sugar until light and fluffy. Add half the egg and beat until well mixed. Stir in the flour and knead the dough with your fingertips to bind it together.

Roll the dough out quite thinly on a well-floured surface and cut out 16 rounds with a 7.5-cm (3-in) biscuit cutter, re-rolling the dough if necessary. Place eight of the rounds at well-spaced intervals on one or more greased baking sheets. Brush the rounds with the remaining beaten egg and position a lollipop stick on each; press another round of dough on top. Bake the biscuits for 15 minutes or until golden and firm. Lift them carefully on to a wire rack to cool.

Colour about two thirds of the glacé icing pale pink or leave it white, as liked, and use it to coat the top of the biscuits. Allow the icing to dry.

Place two coloured sweets on each biscuit for the eyes. Divide the remaining icing into three and colour the portions brown, red and yellow respectively. Using separate piping bags made from greaseproof paper, snip off the tips and pipe mouths, noses, eyelashes and other features on the faces. Allow to dry.

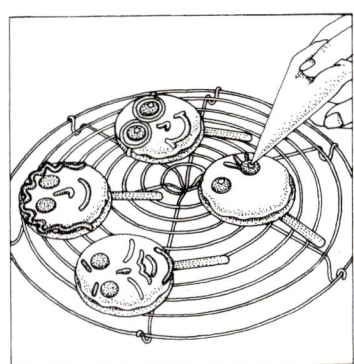

Sunburst patchwork cake

1 (20-cm/8-in) round Light fruit cake (page 24)
Apricot glaze (page 30)
100 g/4 oz flaked almonds, toasted
225 g/8 oz Almond paste (page 31)
food colourings

Brush round the side of the cake with apricot glaze. Scatter the toasted almonds on to a piece of greaseproof paper and, standing the cake on its side, roll it over the almonds to coat the side evenly all over.

Choose or design a pattern for the top of the cake. Place the cake tin upside down on a sheet of paper and draw round it with a pencil. Cut the shape out just inside the pencil outline to give you a round to fit the top of the cake. Fold the round into eight even sections, open it out and draw your pattern on the paper, using a ruler and following the fold marks for guidelines [**1**].

Mark each section of the design with an initial for the colour you intend to use – Y for yellow, O for orange and so on – copy the design on to greaseproof paper and cut out the sections [**2**]. Divide the almond paste into portions, colour each portion as appropriate and roll it out separately. You can use the rust, orange and yellow combination shown here or you can experiment with other colours: pink and green for instance go well together, as do different shades of green and yellow.

Using the templates cut from greaseproof paper and a sharp knife, cut the correct number and shapes of pieces needed for the design from each colour of almond paste [**3**]. Place each piece with its template on one side as soon as you have cut it out to avoid confusion.

Brush the top of the cake with apricot glaze. Carefully lift the cut pieces of almond paste into position, following your original paper pattern for a guide [**4**]. When all the pieces are in place, gently roll over the surface with a rolling pin to smooth the joins [**5**].

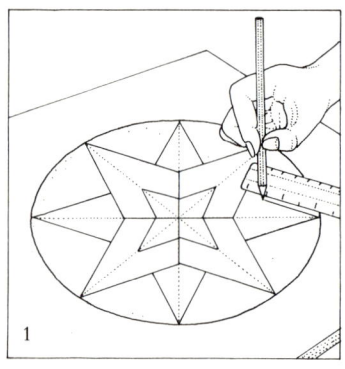
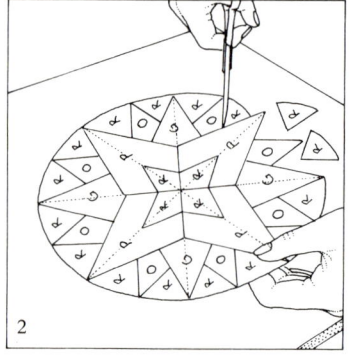
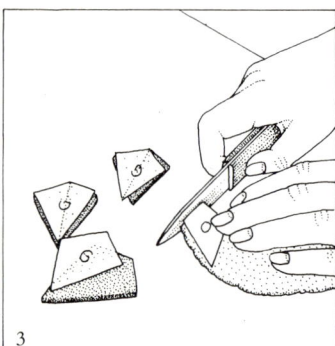
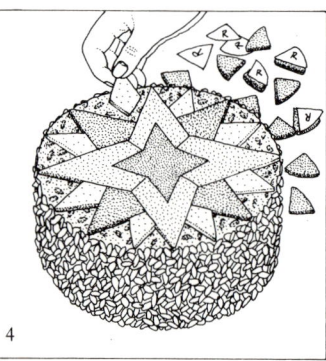
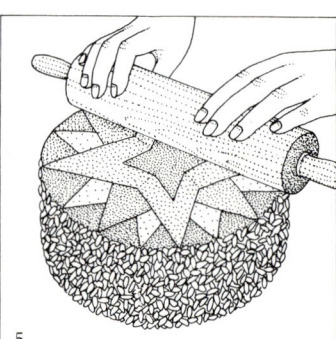

Gingerbread men

Illustrated on page 122

1 quantity Gingerbread mixture (page 26)
1 quantity Glacé icing (page 29)
food colourings

Set the oven at moderate (160 C, 325 F, gas 3). Roll the gingerbread mixture out on a floured surface and cut it into about 30 gingerbread men, using a cutter or the template given on page 54. Arrange the men on greased baking trays and bake them for about 12 minutes or until firm. Lift on to a wire rack to cool.

Divide the glacé icing into three; colour one portion red, one blue and keep the third white. Place some of each colour in a piping bag fitted with a No. 2 plain writing nozzle. Pipe faces and hair on the gingerbread men in white glacé icing and the outline of their jackets in red or blue. Allow the outlines to dry, then fill in each jacket with red or blue icing to match, using a skewer or a fine paint brush. Allow to dry. Finish by piping white buttons down the jackets.

Gingerbread house

Illustrated on page 122

1 quantity Gingerbread mixture (page 26)
450 g / 1 lb Royal icing (page 32)
1 (25-cm/10-in) square silver cake board
assorted coloured sweets to decorate
icing sugar for sprinkling

Draw to scale the end walls, side walls, roof, door and chimney of the gingerbread house on pieces of paper, following the design and measurements given opposite. Cut the pieces out to make your templates.

Bake the gingerbread in two 33 × 23 cm (13 × 9 in) Swiss roll tins following the basic recipe and turn out on to a work surface. Trim the edges with a sharp knife. From one half, cut two end walls and two side walls, positioning the templates on the gingerbread as shown [1]. Cut the two halves of the roof, the chimney and the door from the other half [2]. Stamp out biscuits from any remaining gingerbread or cut out little gingerbread men for the house. Transfer all the pieces to a cooling rack to cool completely.

Mix the royal icing until it is stiff enough to hold well-formed peaks and spread a little on three edges of the side walls and on the bottom edge of each of the end walls. Stick one side wall down on the cake board and position one of the end walls at right-angles to it [3]. Press the edge of the side wall firmly to the end wall to join. Fix the other two walls to the first two in the same way and leave the icing to dry.

Now spread icing along the upper edges of all the walls and carefully fix the two halves of the roof on top, overhanging the walls slightly [4]. Allow to dry.

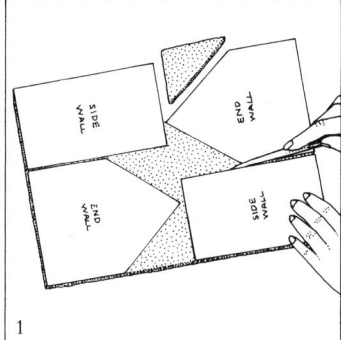

1

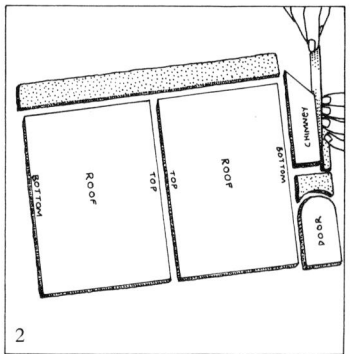

2

CHILDREN'S PARTY CAKES

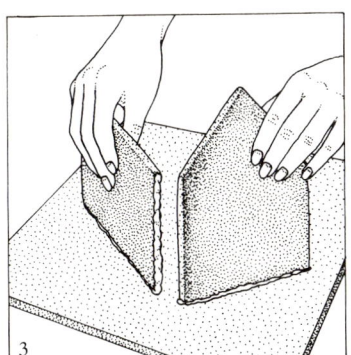
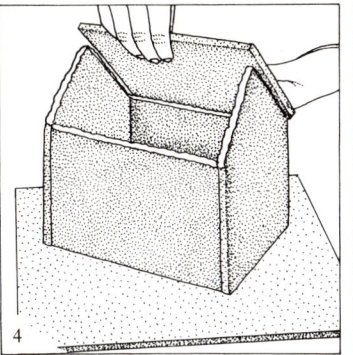
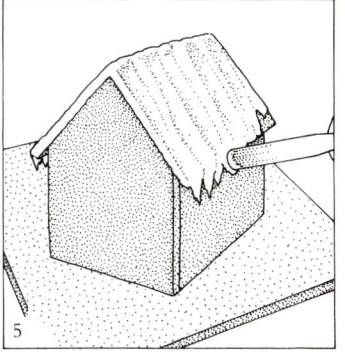

Spread royal icing all over the roof, pulling it down the sides in points to resemble snow and icicles [**5**]. Stick the door and chimney in place with a little more icing. Thin down some icing with water or egg white to a piping consistency and pipe windows on the house and a door knob, using a No. 2 plain writing nozzle. While the icing is still wet, stick coloured sweets over the roof and on the cake board, if liked. Sprinkle icing sugar lightly over the house and board to give a snowy effect and leave to dry.

Overleaf: Gingerbread house
Gingerbread men

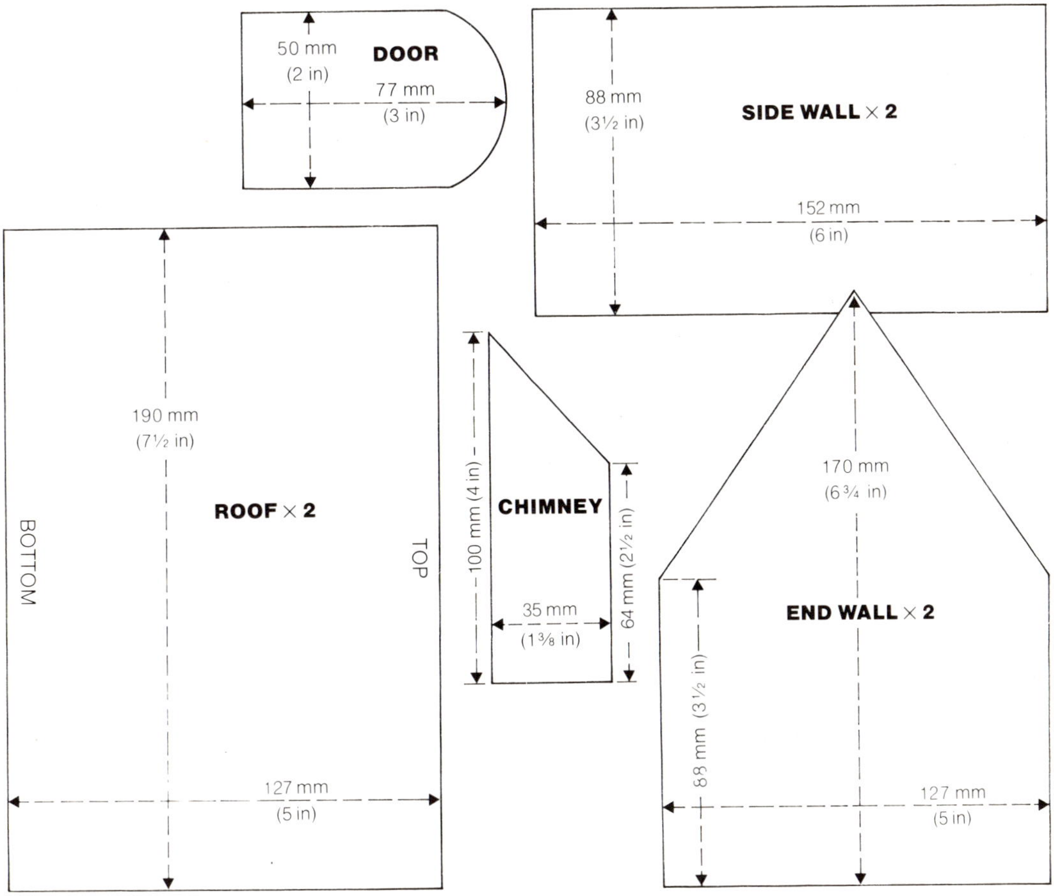

DOOR
50 mm (2 in)
77 mm (3 in)

SIDE WALL × 2
88 mm (3½ in)
152 mm (6 in)

ROOF × 2
190 mm (7½ in)
127 mm (5 in)
BOTTOM
TOP

CHIMNEY
100 mm (4 in)
35 mm (1⅜ in)
64 mm (2½ in)

END WALL × 2
170 mm (6¾ in)
88 mm (3½ in)
127 mm (5 in)

Index

Almond and fondant petits fours 110
Almond paste 31; to apply to a cake 38–9; to colour 47
Almond paste decorations 47–8
American frosting 30
American wedding cake 98
Angel, template for an 55
Apple (modelled in almond paste) 48
Apricot glaze 30

Basket or ribbon nozzle 16
Bell, template for a 55
Birthday cakes:
 Buttercup birthday cake 76
 Eighteenth birthday cake 74
 Numeral birthday cake 73
 Primrose birthday cake 73
 Twenty-first birthday cake 93
Biscuits:
 Funny face lollipop biscuits 117
 Gingerbread men 120
 Iced peanut biscuits 117
Black Forest gâteau 69
Boiled fondant icing 33–4
Butter icing or butter cream 28; to use 38
Buttercup birthday cake 76
Butterfly wedding cake 100–1

Cake cards, cake boards 14
Cake tins 19; to prepare 20
Cakes, basic. See also Birthday, Celebration, Children's party cakes etc.
 Basic one-stage sandwich 21
 Basic Victoria sandwich 21
 Basic whisked sponge 22
 Chocolate sandwich cake 21
 Chocolate Swiss roll 23
 Coffee sandwich cake 21
 Farmhouse fruit cake 26
 Genoese sponge 22
 Gingerbread 26
 Lemon sandwich cake 21
 Light fruit cake 24
 Nut sandwich cake 21
 Orange sandwich cake 21
 Rich fruit cake 24–5
 Spice sandwich cake 21
 Swiss roll 23
Caramel American frosting 30
Caramel fudge icing 29
Caraque, to make 50
Celebration cakes:
 Birthday cakes 73–6
 Christmas cakes 84–91
 Easter cake 80
 Harvest basket 82
 Mother's Day cake 77
 Simnel cake 81
 Strawberry Valentine cake 77
Children's party cakes:
 Chocolate train cake 116
 Drum cake 114
 Gingerbread house 120–1
 Parcel cake 112–13
 Sunburst patchwork cake 118
Chocolate:
 To comb chocolate 51
 To cut chocolate shapes 51
 To make caraque 50
 To make chocolate curls 50
 To make chocolate leaves 51
 To melt chocolate 50
 To pipe chocolate shapes 51
 Black Forest gâteau 69
 Chocolate butter icing 28
 Chocolate crème au beurre 28
 Chocolate fudge icing 29
 Chocolate glacé icing 29
 Chocolate peppermint swirl 68
 Chocolate rum sandwich 69
 Chocolate sandwich cake 21
 Chocolate Swiss roll 23
 Chocolate train cake 116
 Chocolate yule log 84
 Iced chocolate square 72
 Types of chocolate 50
Christening cakes:
 Crib christening cake 106
 Daisy christening cake 104

Christmas cakes:
 Chocolate yule log 84
 Christmas bell cake 85
 Light Christmas cake 84
 Poinsettia Christmas cake 90
 Robin redbreast Christmas cake 88–9
 Snowman Christmas cake 86
Christmas rose (modelled in fondant icing) 49
Christmas tree, template for a 55
Citrus ring 65
Coffee:
 Coffee American frosting 30
 Coffee banana slice 66
 Coffee butter icing 28
 Coffee crème au beurre 28
 Coffee fudge icing 29
 Coffee glacé icing 29
 Coffee sandwich cake 21
 Coffee walnut gâteau 72
Combing chocolate 51
Containers 14
Couverture 50
Covers for bowls 14
Crème au beurre 28
Crib christening cake 106
Crystallised lemon slices 62
Crystallising flowers 52
Cup cakes (lemon) 68

Daffodil (modelled in fondant icing) 49
Daisy christening cake 104
Daisy, to pipe a 45
Dove, template for a 54
Drum cake 114

Easter cake 80
Easter chicks (modelled in almond paste) 81
Eighteenth birthday cake 74
Engagement cake 92
Equipment 13–14; special for icing 14–18; care of 18

Fabric icing bag, to use 36
Farmhouse fruit cake 26
Father Christmas (modelled in almond paste) 48

Father Christmas, template for a 55
Feather-iced sandwich cake 61
Feather icing 37
Fillings see Icings and fillings
Flat icing 40–1
Flooding with glacé icing 37
Flower nail 17
Flowers:
 To crystallise 52
 To model in almond paste 48
 To model in fondant icing 49
 To pipe flowers 45
 Template for flowers 55
Fondant icing:
 Boiled fondant icing 33–4
 Kneaded fondant icing 34
 Modelling with fondant icing 49
Formal cakes:
 Christening cakes 104, 106
 Engagement cake 92
 Golden wedding cake 109
 Iced fancies 105
 Silver wedding cake 108
 Twenty-first birthday cake 93
 Wedding cakes 96–103
Frosted caramel roll 65
Frosting see American frosting
Fruit:
 Farmhouse fruit cake 26
 Fruit crème au beurre 28
 Fruits modelled in almond paste 48
 Light fruit cake 24
 Rich fruit cake 24–5
 Teatime fruit ring 61
Fudge icing 29
Funny face lollipop biscuits 117

Gâteaux:
 Black Forest gâteau 69
 Chocolate rum sandwich 69
 Coffee walnut gâteau 72
 Iced chocolate square 72
 Pineapple ginger slice 70
Genoese sponge 22
Gingerbread 26
Gingerbread house 120–1

INDEX

Gingerbread men 120; template for 54
Glacé-iced sponge 60
Glacé icing 29; flooding with 37
Golden wedding cake 109
Grapes (modelled in almond paste) 48
Greaseproof icing bag, to make 15; to use 36
Greetings, templates for 56

Harvest basket 82
Heart, template for a 54
Holly leaves (modelled in almond paste) 47

Iced chocolate square 72
Iced fancies 105
Iced peanut biscuits 117
Icing bags 14–15, to use 36
Icing comb 17
Icing moulds 17
Icing nails 17
Icing ruler 17
Icing syringes 16
Icings and fillings:
　Almond paste 31
　American frosting 30
　Boiled fondant icing 33–4
　Butter icing or butter cream 28
　Caramel American frosting 30
　Caramel fudge icing 29
　Chocolate butter icing 28
　Chocolate crème au beurre 28
　Chocolate fudge icing 29
　Chocolate glacé icing 29
　Coffee American frosting 30
　Coffee butter icing 28
　Coffee crème au beurre 28
　Coffee fudge icing 29
　Coffee glacé icing 29
　Crème au beurre 28
　Fruit crème au beurre 28
　Fudge icing 29
　Glacé icing 29
　Kneaded fondant 34
　Lemon American frosting 30
　Lemon butter icing 28
　Lemon crème au beurre 28
　Lemon fudge icing 29
　Lemon glacé icing 29
　Liqueur butter icing 28
　Liqueur crème au beurre 28
　Liqueur glacé icing 29

　Orange American frosting 30
　Orange butter icing 28
　Orange crème au beurre 28
　Orange fudge icing 29
　Orange glacé icing 29
　Royal icing 32
　Seven-minute frosting 30
　Vanilla butter icing 28
Ivory wedding cake 97

Key, template for a 55
Kneaded fondant 34

Lace-edged wedding cake 102
Lacy sponge, quick 58
Lattice sponge 60
Leaves:
　Almond paste leaves 47
　Chocolate leaves 51
Lemon:
　Crystallised lemon slices 62
　Lemon American frosting 30
　Lemon butter icing 28
　Lemon crème au beurre 28
　Lemon cup cakes 68
　Lemon fudge icing 29
　Lemon fudge loaf 62
　Lemon glacé icing 29
　Lemon (modelled in almond paste) 48
　Lemon sandwich cake 21
　Lemon sunflower cake 64
Lettering in run-out technique 47
Light Christmas cake 84
Light fruit cake 24
Lime (modelled in almond paste) 48
Liqueur butter icing 28
Liqueur crème au beurre 28
Liqueur glacé icing 29

Marking rings and wedges 17
Mixers and beaters 13
Mixing bowls 13
Modelling with almond paste 48; with fondant icing 49
Mother's Day cake 77

Name plates, templates for 53
Nozzles 15–16
Numeral birthday cake 73
Numerals in run-out techniques 47
Numerals, templates for 56
Nut sandwich cake 21

One-stage sandwich, basic 21

Orange:
　Orange American frosting 30
　Orange butter icing 28
　Orange crème au beurre 28
　Orange feather-iced sandwich cake 61
　Orange fudge icing 29
　Orange glacé icing 29
　Orange modelled in almond paste 48
　Orange sandwich cake 21

Palette knife 13
Parcel cake 112–13
Pastry brush 14
Pear (modelled in almond paste) 48
Petal nozzle 16
Petits fours 110
Pineapple ginger slice 70
Piping chocolate shapes 51
Piping techniques 43–5
Plastic icing bag, to use 36
Poinsettia Christmas cake 90
Primrose birthday cake 73

Rabbit, template for a 54
Ribbon nozzle 16
Robin redbreast Christmas cake 88–9
Rolling pin 13
Rose:
　Modelled in almond paste 48
　Piped rose 45
　Rose trellis wedding cake 96
Rough icing 41
Royal icing 32; to apply 40–1
Run-outs, to make 46–7

Sandwich cakes 21
Scallops, template for 53
Seven-minute frosting 30
Shell nozzle 16; to use 43
Sieve 13
Silver wedding cake 108
Simnel cake 81
Snowman Christmas cake 86
Spatula 13
Spice sandwich cake 21
Spoons 13
Star nozzle 16; to use 43
Stars, template for 53
Stock syrup for boiled fondant 34
Strawberry (modelled in almond paste) 48
Strawberry Valentine cake 77
Sugar thermometer 18

Sunburst patchwork cake 118
Swiss rolls 23

Tea time cakes:
　Chocolate peppermint swirl 68
　Citrus ring 65
　Coffee banana slice 66
　Frosted caramel roll 65
　Glacé-iced sponge 60
　Lattice sponge 60
　Lemon cup cakes 68
　Lemon fudge loaf 62
　Lemon sunflower cake 64
　Orange feather-iced sandwich cake 61
　Quick lacy sponge 58
　Teatime fruit ring 61
Template designs 53–6
Templates 17–18; to make 42
Trellis piping 44
Triangle, template for a 53
Turntables 14
Twenty-first birthday cake 93

Valentine cakes:
　Strawberry Valentine cake 77
Vanilla butter icing 28
Victoria sandwich, basic 21

Wedding cakes:
　American wedding cake 98
　Butterfly wedding cake 100–1
　Ivory wedding cake 97
　Lace-edged wedding cake 102
　Rose trellis wedding cake 96
Whisked sponge, basic 22
Writing nozzles 16
Writing in run-out technique 47

Yule log (chocolate) 84

ACKNOWLEDGEMENTS

The publishers would like to thank Metal Box Limited for supplying the Tala icing utensils used in this book. Further enquiries for the full range of Tala equipment should be sent to:

The Anne Anson Advisory Bureau,
Consumer Products Division,
Metal Box Limited,
Oddicroft Lane,
Sutton-in-Ashfield
Nottinghamshire.
NG17 5FS

USEFUL ADDRESSES

A varied range of cake icing equipment and decorations can also be obtained from the stockists and manufacturers listed below. Write for details of catalogues and prices.

Mary Ford Cake Artistry Centre
28–30, Southbourne Grove
Bournemouth
Dorset
BH6 3RA

Baker Smith Cake Decorators Limited
65, The Street
Tongham
Farnham
Surrey
GU10 1DD

G. T. Culpitt and Son Limited
P.O. Box 77
Culpitt House
74–78, Town Centre
Hatfield
Hertfordshire
AL10 0AW

Anniversary House Limited
23–25 Abbott Road
Winton
Bournemouth
Dorset
BH9 1EY

Kitchen Devils
Wilkinson Sword Limited
Sword House
Totteridge Road
High Wycombe
Buckinghamshire
HP13 6EJ

Covent Garden Kitchen Supplies
3 North Row
The Market
Covent Garden
London WC2

B. R. Mathews and Son
12 Gypsy Hill
London
SE19 1NN

Felicity Clare
Felicity House
Preston Road
Clayton-le-woods
Chorley
Lancashire
PR6 7EH